GET RICH
OR LIE
TRYING

Symeon Brown is a reporter and journalist at Channel 4 News. He was shortlisted for an Orwell Prize in 2019 and shortlisted at the 2018 British Journalism Awards. He has written for a range of media including Vice, the *Guardian*, Huffington Post, CNN, *New Statesman* and The Voice.

GET RICH OR LIE TRYING

Ambition and Deceit in the New Influencer Economy

SYMEON BROWN

Atlantic Books
London

First published in Great Britain in 2022 by Atlantic Books,
an imprint of Atlantic Books Ltd.

This paperback edition published in 2023.

10 9 8 7 6 5 4 3 2 1

A CIP catalogue record for this book is available from the British Library.

Paperback ISBN: 978-1-83895-030-9
E-book ISBN: 978-1-83895-029-3

Printed in Great Britain by Clays Ltd, Elcograf S.p.A.

Atlantic Books
An imprint of Atlantic Books Ltd
Ormond House
26–27 Boswell Street
London
WC1N 3JZ

www.atlantic-books.co.uk

CONTENTS

INTRODUCTION

———

THE HUSTLER'S AMBITION

I was a 14-year-old schoolboy when the rapper 50 Cent released *Get Rich or Die Tryin'*. The most precocious kids in class declared the debut hip-hop album an instant classic and hailed the rapper's legend: 'He's been shot nine times, you know?' The narrowly failed attempt on 50 Cent's life was at the centre of his sales pitch as the bulletproof king of gangsta rap. My friends and I were easily sold – and far from the only ones. Fifty's debut was the best-selling album of 2003. It sold 872,000 copies in the first week, and 12 million copies worldwide by the end of the year.[1] Curtis '50 Cent' Jackson may have been born black and poor in New York, but he was now worth more than a few cents from selling his rags-to-riches tale to a world that loves an underdog.

There are few things we find more compelling than a fable of overcoming the odds and achieving self-made success. Everyone loves an outsider, because deep down most of us believe we are one, and each generation has its own version for inspiration. For my churchgoing grandmother, the scrappy underdog was exemplified by the biblical story of a shepherd boy named David defeating the giant Goliath. For me, it was the constant reinvention of the hustler made good in hip-hop that stuck.

When I bought *Get Rich or Die Tryin'* with the meagre change I'd saved from my paper round, hip-hop had replaced rock as America's most listened-to genre and the rest of the world was not far behind. In the videos broadcast on MTV Base, rappers like 50 Cent would display the full trappings of their new and often exaggerated wealth, with the deprived neighbourhoods they came from as a backdrop. The credo of commercial hip-hop set in this era was that hustling, vice and the music of the streets comprised the underground railroad to freedom. Poverty was worse than death, so you had two choices: get rich or die trying. If the system wasn't fair, work around it.

At 15 years old, DeAndre Cortez Way, now better known as Soulja Boy, was a young rapper without a powerful marketing story like 50 Cent's. He had no record deal, no publicist, and no industry behind him, but none of that mattered. He had LimeWire. The site was used by millennials across the world to upload and download music illegally. DeAndre would upload his music and name his tracks after 50 Cent songs so that people trying to bootleg 50 Cent's music would find themselves listening to Soulja Boy's instead.[2] This trick earned him attention, and the teenager had more up his sleeve.

In the early days of social media, Cortez Way was using it in a way that was as alien then as it is familiar now. He linked his MySpace to a young social media site called YouTube and, using the buzz generated through mislabelling his own music, gained millions of online listens. His breakout song, 'Crank That', went viral in 2007 with the aid of a gimmicky dance, and made the teenager a reported $7m.[3] Soulja Boy had, by design or good fortune, created a formula for viral success that is still being used today by artists, companies and social media influencers. The hip-hop magazine *Vibe* called him 'a new millennium hustler with a web army'[4] recruited by misleading people to his music. If get rich or die trying was the formula of the crack dealer turned rapper, then get rich or *lie* trying might describe the new modus operandi for the twenty-first century, especially among the millions now deploying Soulja Boy's playbook to capture the internet's attention and grow huge online fandoms.

There are now millions of people making a living from their digital followings. This book, the result of an investigation that has spanned years, is a journey into their world. I met streamers, marketers, tech entrepreneurs, sex workers, dropshippers and fraudsters. I saw how easily ambition transforms itself into deceit online and how social media has emerged as the most exploitative frontier of late-stage capitalism. I heard extraordinary tales of exploitation, delusion, dishonesty and chutzpah. And the more people I encountered, the more I started to see how much this brave new world had in common with the one we all know so well.

Fame and fortune

I grew up in Tottenham, north London, a multiracial area between the City and the Hertfordshire suburbs with a character defined by its then underperforming football club and its Caribbean, Ghanaian and Turkish Cypriot communities. My whole life, this corner of the city has been notorious for the anti-police riots that broke out in the 1980s. A Jamaican-born mother had died after her home was raided by police officers, a policeman was killed in the ensuing revolt, and the tension between the residents and the authorities has festered ever since.

By 2003, much of the area could have slipped with ease into the background of a rap video in Queens. My friends and I wore American hip-hop streetwear: baggy Akademiks jeans, FUBU tops and Timberland boots. New Era baseball caps felt like part of our school uniform. Aylward School was made up of the children – or in my case the grandchildren – of migrants, alongside the remnants of London's white working class who for years had been gradually moving away from the centre of London. The school had a high intake of students poor enough to qualify for free school meals. My teacher described it as an outer-city school with inner-city problems and a revolving door of staff. In the year I completed my GCSEs, 75 per cent of my fellow students failed to get the five A*–C grades necessary to go on to further education. It is unsurprising that the hustler in hip-hop was a relatable figure of inspiration to a student body of underdogs.

The genre's vulgar representations of women and unapologetic aggression may have offended the sensibilities of middle-class America and Britain, but the young black men in baggy jeans and tank tops were putting into verse what Wall Street's old white men in pinstripe suits had been preaching for decades. It was ostentatious, ruthless, violent, entrepreneurial, aspirational, individualistic and unwilling to play by the rules. These values are America's most influential global export, and across the Atlantic, my friends and I were part of a generation unable to escape it.

We were the final cohort of students in Britain to enter secondary school in the last millennium, and as such were dubbed 'millennials', a word applied to the generation born between 1980 and 1996. That may have conjured up images of a limitless future, but whatever we needed to succeed in this brave new world was not provided at Aylward, a school ranked consistently near the bottom of the league table and failing to get its new students fit for the twenty-first century. The very month I entered it, Prime Minister Tony Blair, 18 months in power, laid out the challenge facing the generation 'at the frontier of the new millennium' in a speech to Labour's 1999 autumn conference:

> A spectre haunts the world: technological revolution. Ten years ago, a fifteen-year-old probably couldn't work a computer. Now he's in danger of living on it. Over a trillion dollars traded every day in currency markets and with them the fate of nations. Global finance and communications and media. Electronic commerce. The Internet … Every year a new revolution scattering in its wake, security, and ways of living for millions of people.[5]

These were the forces of change driving the future of a new knowledge-based economy, said Blair. His government's policy ambition was to raise the number of adult graduates. This would further the precipitous increase of recent decades (from 3.4 per cent in 1950 to 19.8 per cent in 1990),[6] following the growth in polytechnics and the Open University aimed at the aspirational working classes.

Economists believe that advanced literacy has a profound impact on the way a nation views itself and shapes the expectations citizens have for their lives. Two generations earlier, my mum, the British-born daughter of Jamaican migrants, had been discouraged by her teachers from even applying for university. Today, it is seen as a prerequisite for any decent job (and many mediocre ones). My school careers adviser would tell us to apply to any university we could, quoting estimates that graduates would earn between £170,000 and £250,000 more than non-grads over a lifetime.[7] The message was that the prospects of the haves and the have-nots would no longer be determined by what our parents did for a living, or by Britain's ingrained class system. Our future success would now depend on our level of education, with a little room for some aspiration as well.

It was not long before 'aspiration' itself became an entrenched political buzzword, and if you were failing, it was due to the absence of that magical dust. When there were outbreaks of violence in urban communities like mine, the government blamed a lack of drive, and in 2006, it launched the Reach mentoring scheme, with the focus on 'raising the aspirations and achievement among Black boys and young Black men, enabling them to achieve their potential'.[8] Ten years later, white working-class young men from post-industrial towns were diagnosed as being severely under-represented in higher education, and the Conservative education secretary told universities that they needed to help 'raise the aspiration' of 'white British disadvantaged children',[9] as if aspiration was the only thing the underdog needed to succeed. The problem, certainly in my neighbourhood, was that it was aspiration itself, rather than the absence of it, that drove young men to desperate measures.

In my early teens, I was befriended by a boy who lived a few roads over from me. Eugene was light brown, with a boxed high-top and a reputation for fighting, and went by the nickname 'Fatman'. He was probably only a year older than me, but he towered above me. One day, he took a curious interest in me before deciding I was 'safe' enough to offer me a 'job'. 'Are you interested in making some money and shotting [selling weed] for me?' he asked. Although I declined, many others didn't. Several weeks later, Fatman was stabbed to death.

The drug trade is notoriously violent but still manages to recruit a conveyor belt of young men desperate to be someone only to find themselves trapped after falling for the promise of a loyal family and an easy income. Such benefits rarely materialise, but the trade is nevertheless a rational choice for teenagers who have often failed in education when it is exalted as the only route to a good job.

In recent decades, aspiration has been heavily wrapped up not in what we aim to do, achieve or create but in what we can afford to buy. Young adults and teenagers have been under more and more pressure to be successful with fewer means to do so. Brands have aggressively told us that the road to contentment is through consumption. In my school, those on free school meals still wore luxury streetwear. Today, brands like Gucci are ubiquitous in school playgrounds across Britain and North America. In 2019, Kering, the company that owns Gucci and other luxury brands, posted record revenue and operating margins, making over €15bn.[10] The pressure to dress for success and fake it till you make it is overwhelming. While social media has accelerated this trend, it did not create it.

Even before I became a teenager, the pressure to succeed was inescapable no matter where I was: at school, on the streets or even at church. The get-rich doctrine was more than an ideology; it was a literal gospel that had a knack for sweeping up black converts, including my mum. My mother and I attended a mostly Nigerian congregation in east London. The evangelical services were theatrical productions, led by a middle-aged man with an impeccably sharp high-top fade and a well-cut suit who spoke in a transatlantic lilt somewhere between Lagosian and New Yorker. Pastor Matthew was a charismatic performer too. He moved around the stage like a well-trained MC, able to skilfully speed up or slow down the pace and volume of his oratory for dramatic effect.

The church grew rapidly by word of mouth, with the pastor encouraging the congregation to make referrals. 'Invite someone you know to church,' he would end his sermons with, just after collecting financial tithes. The invitation system worked, but what really boosted attendance each Sunday was Pastor Matthew's growing fame. Soon he would have over 10,000 people sitting before him on a single Sunday, generating millions in revenue a year. His sermons were televised on Christian satellite channels that made celebrities out of the most telegenic American performers. Pastor Matthew was part reverend, part business coach, who told his congregation to aspire to the mindset of the rich to 'increase your yield', as God did not want his followers to be poor. He promised that giving money to those above you was a way to 'sow a seed' and achieve a life of abundance.

The growing desire for fame and wealth among the old working class was part of the political landscape defined by Tony Blair's crushing electoral victory in 1997 over John Major's incumbent Conservative Party, ending their almost 20 years in power. In that time, the might of the financial markets had been unleashed, manufacturing was in decline and inequality had spiralled.

New Labour's pitch was taken from Bill Clinton's Democrats, built on an ease with the wealthy but a discomfort with a workforce unequipped for the new millennium. The Labour Party took power on International Workers' Day, but Blair's New Labour had abandoned the traditional collectivism of its trade union roots in favour of the individual self-invention first globalised by Ronald

Reagan. A man more telegenic and entrepreneurial than any televangelist, Blair admired the rich and the famous and presented himself as the country's biggest star. His ascent to power was one of several events in 1997 that hinted at where Western society was headed.

First, there was our infatuation with celebrity, embodied in the premature death of Princess Diana. The princess who had traded in her royalty for superstardom was killed being pursued by cameramen hell-bent on feeding our insatiable appetite for unattainable glamour and beauty. A month earlier, Diana had attended the funeral of murdered designer Gianni Versace, who had arguably reinvented both. In the words of the *Guardian*'s associate fashion editor, Versace had 'put fashion in the middle of a new celebrity solar system and clothes at the centre of popular culture', as high fashion became an aspiration for ordinary men and women.[11]

In March 1997, the hip-hop star Notorious B.I.G., who was instrumental in making Versace popular, was murdered following a fatal feud between East and West Coast gangs that had already been responsible for the death of Tupac Shakur a year earlier. The drama gripped fans of hip-hop like reality TV and drew an international audience. The beef may have cost the scene its biggest icons, but the attention from their martyrdom was instrumental in hip-hop's transition into the twenty-first century's most-listened-to genre, which to this day still preaches Biggie's mantra of 'fuck bitches, get money'.

The hysteria caused by the premature deaths of Diana, Versace and Biggie represented the new holy trinity of fame: high society (Diana), ostentatious celebrities (Versace) and the self-made famous with a story to sell (Biggie).

This was also the year Steve Jobs returned to Apple, in a second coming that would presage unprecedented success for the company and herald a new era of tech oligarchy. Apple has been transformed from a company selling computers into a way of life for millennials, with as much brand loyalty as some religions. The impact of the iPhone alone is proof that this is no exaggeration. Apple stock ended 1997 at 0.56 cents a share. As of writing, the value of the company has increased by a staggering 127,647 per cent. By 2019, Apple's revenues were larger than the entire GDP of Portugal.[12]

Companies like Apple rose in stature as once-powerful countries declined. When Blair took office, his first major foreign gesture was to hand Hong Kong back to China. This marked the end of Britain's imperial project in a world where the new power was being exercised by tech companies with more money and influence than entire nations. In this globalised world order, money was power, and for Blair what mattered was ensuring individuals were equipped to make it. Today, all they need is a smartphone and access to Instagram or TikTok.

A rigged economy

In the 2000s, teenagers would dial up to use the internet and speak to friends on instant messaging services like MSN. Some of the era's internet slang is just about still used (LOL), but phrases like BRB (be right back) are out of date because nobody is ever offline. Our internet habits slowly morphed from congregating around a desktop to keeping a more powerful mobile computer in our palms 24/7. With it, new avenues of seemingly limitless riches presented themselves.

No single invention has created more wealth than the internet. Thirty years ago, the Forbes list featured the planet's biggest industrialists, and even drug dealers: Pablo Escobar made the list seven years in a row.[13] Today, the dope cartels have been drowned out by the wealth of internet kingpins like Jeff Bezos and Mark Zuckerberg. Although the respective creators of Amazon and Facebook have more money than God, the lure of success has also trickled down to even the poorest neighbourhoods in the world, with the advent of social media.

It was not just teenage musicians who migrated to YouTube to set up channels or accounts and invited the world into their lives. We all did, bringing with us a wide array of hobbies and interests: make-up, gaming, sport, the markets, travel, politics, celebrity gossip and fitness.

You name it, there are now thousands of channels for it, run by professionals and enthusiastic hobbyists alike. As millions of us clicked to take a voyeuristic interest in the mundane affairs of ordinary people, we wrested power away from the mass media that had once had a monopoly on our attention. In the process, we generated a new global currency: influence.

Over the past century, political parties and brands have spent endless sums of money to gain our attention and influence our decisions. Today, that attention is increasingly in the hands of a new type of hustler. An influencer is a figure who by accident or design has gained thousands or even millions of social media followers and converted their following into an income by making their feeds a living billboard or a peep show you pay to subscribe to if you are a superfan.

Ten years ago, this pseudo-profession did not even exist, and yet now millions of children, teenagers and adults are trying to go viral and capture our attention in a dogfight for followers, fame and, ultimately, fortune. The highest-earning influencer, Kylie Jenner, can earn up to $1.2m from a single post on Instagram,[14] yet not all influencers want cash or are even selling products. Popularity on the internet, better known as 'clout', can also open doors. Whether we have 200,000 followers or 200, the rewards from a social media presence encourage us to represent ourselves in a way that is beneficial to us. Whether that means beefing up our employment history to prospective employers on LinkedIn, expressing outrage on Twitter to appear enlightened, or airbrushing our photos to get more likes, social media encourages us to glamorise ourselves and misrepresent our reality as it introduces a profit motive into our social lives, with a profound impact on the way we behave.

Since I left university, the economic promise made to middle-class millennials has gone to shit. In 2008, I was an economics undergraduate learning about how boom and bust had been banished. We all know what happened next: the global economy crashed. Graduate schemes disappeared before my eyes and the next decade did not live up to the promises made in the one before. Those of us born between 1980 and 1996 became the first post-war generation set to do worse than our parents, despite being better educated.[15] In real terms, 30-year-olds today in the US and UK earn less than they did 20 years ago, and the cost of living has increased to such an extent that it is common in many Western countries to house-share deep into our thirties.[16] Home ownership for the under-forties has collapsed, yet advertising has never been more aggressive. Our consumer spending is higher and personal debt has rocketed.[17] And this was before the COVID-19 Armageddon struck and making money from home became the only game in town.

It is in this climate that 'influencing' seems a viable career, providing a potentially luxury lifestyle with a low entry threshold. You don't need a top degree or a well-connected uncle; you merely need to gain the internet's attention. Then you can monetise yourself as both product and salesman. Often we do not even think of the most successful influencers as digital workers, since they market themselves as relationship gurus, financial experts and activists. Some influencers even offer teaching on how you can emulate their success. One super-YouTuber named Patricia Bright, who has over 2.6m subscribers, has written a book titled *Heart & Hustle*, which promises 'to show you how to hustle like I do'.

The problem is that success in this world is not as attainable as some make it seem, and the addictive rewards of accruing followers by any means necessary are warping human behaviour both on- and offline. In the past, ostentatious displays of wealth came from rappers and film stars. Today, they feed into our smartphones all day from our peers and from celebrities who are famous just for being themselves. In December 2021, *Love Island*'s Molly-Mae told the *Diary of a CEO* podcast that, 'You're given one life and it's down to you what you do with it… if you want something enough, you can achieve it.' But for every Molly-Mae or Kylie Jenner, there are millions who struggle to gain a foothold. In a world where glitter is presented as gold, this book sets out to tell the stories behind the glitz and the glamour.

For influencers, deception is lucrative and becoming increasingly extreme. There are those feigning their wealth, their followers and even their ethnicity while hawking dubious products to their followers. In recent years influencers have sold laxatives as health drinks, promoted disastrous music festivals that never happened and been caught up in serious fraud and multimillion-dollar Ponzi schemes. Companies that sell regulated products like cosmetic surgery procedures and financial services have increasingly turned to morally ambivalent influencers to market their goods to vulnerable consumers, away from the watchful eye of the authorities. Influencing may soon be the internet's most saturated hustle, but it is one that on closer inspection looks like a giant pyramid scheme. Its real beneficiaries – the companies and shareholders reaping the highest rewards – are hidden by those desperate to take centre stage.

1

THE UNICORN IN POLYESTER

On the surface, Panorama City in LA does not look like the birthplace of a billion-dollar tech company. Once home to a mighty General Motors assembly plant, today it is a down-at-heel neighbourhood, home to a predominantly immigrant community made up of Armenians, Filipinos and Latinos. At its centre, where the factory used to reside, is the Panorama Mall. As in many post-industrial communities, a huge site of production has been replaced by a centre of mass consumption. Inside, however, is the home of one of the digital era's most unlikely success stories and most influential businesses, one the average white man over 30 has never heard of.

Hidden in a row of costume-jewellery sellers and outlets offering cash to punters with poor credit is Fashion Nova, which could soon prove to be a unicorn (a billion-dollar company). It may not be a tech company in the way

Facebook or Microsoft is. It does not produce software or rely on algorithms. However, its entire success is built on its dominance of social media and modern internet culture. The company has been instrumental in creating a new model of women's work, and has cemented the twenty-first century's new beauty ideals anywhere American pop culture dominates.

Fashion Nova's impact could not have been predicted when its first store was opened in 2006 at Panorama Mall by the company's founder, an industrious Iranian-American named Richard Saghian. Saghian may not be a household name like Gianni Versace or Calvin Klein, but his brand has been far more revolutionary in the Instagram era, despite only setting up a website as late as 2013. When the first Fashion Nova store opened, the company was unrecognisable from the one that made it the most googled fashion brand 12 years later. Its humble roots are still visible in Panorama City Mall, where the Fashion Nova store is painted a basic white. The floor is tiled like a public bath-room and the decor has no hint of glamour. It feels like a low-budget outlet store, and the prices match. No item costs much more than $34.99, and when I visit, I am the only man among a dozen customers and staff, all of whom are young Latina or African-American women with fuller figures, many sporting surgically enhanced backsides. The store plays hip-hop stripper anthems by Fetty Wap and

Cardi B, a former exotic dancer turned megastar who is also a paid ambassador for the brand.

The music played in store complements the aesthetic of the skimpy clothes that have made Fashion Nova a market leader in ghetto chic and timeless hoochie wear. You can buy similar styles in the store next door, an unbranded clothes shop called Mode Plus, or the budget womenswear shop opposite, called Queens (the menswear shop next door is Kings). The same tight party dresses produced by undocumented migrants for cents and sold for dollars are for sale in all of them, and can be found in any other makeshift store in low-income Latina communities from Panorama City in LA to my native Tottenham in north London. However, Fashion Nova has come a long way from the humble store in the Panorama City Mall. Richard Saghian may have had textiles in his blood – his father ran a womenswear store he worked in himself – but he knew the world was changing, and that if he was going to succeed, he would have to change as well. His first step was to hire people who could show him how.

Bimi Fafowora, the daughter of a civil engineer and an ophthalmologist, was studying sociology with marketing when she saw a post from a small fashion company advertising a vacancy in their marketing team. Stereotypically, children of middle-class Nigerians living in Europe or America are under pressure to achieve professional success as doctors or lawyers, but Bimi had always been creative at heart. Outside of her studies, she photographed young women with modelling ambitions, and when she saw the job advert, she fired off her portfolio.

She was invited to bring her ideas to a meeting with the big boss, Richard, in Northridge. 'I presented to him some plans to clean up their marketing and brand aesthetic, and I was taken on from there.' It was an important break for 22-year-old Bimi. 'At the time I didn't think of it as a big deal because Fashion Nova were not as big as they are now,' she said coolly. 'I grew up in the Valley. I just knew it as a store that was at the mall.' Back then, she remembered the store selling everything from school uniforms to casual wear. The company had only just launched its website, and one of her tasks was to help update it and create the company's first list of attractive and popular Instagram influencers to send clothes to.

Bimi's upper-middle-class tastes clashed with Richard's street-culture instincts, but she soon caught on. Richard wanted his company to target the kind of curvaceous girls who went to clubs to dance to hip-hop and desired to be on a VIP table – sexy girls who were happy for their sex appeal to be consumed and wanted to be famous. Most importantly, they had to be able to turn heads on Instagram.

The company began recruiting micro-famous brand ambassadors who fitted the vision. Young women with big followings were given free clothes, and those with huge ones were paid a fee to post. They were told to always tag Fashion Nova to help its followers grow and boost awareness. Some ambassadors were also allowed to earn money from selling clothes using a discount code that paid them a commission. Where the company achieved major success was in its aggressive penetration of the hip-hop scene. It paid rappers for a shout-out on songs and signed up artists like the reality TV star turned rap superstar Cardi B to be highly-paid brand ambassadors. It even gave the African-American and Latin entertainers who now dominate American pop culture their own Fashion Nova lines. The company had bought a seat at the table. But it also stole scraps from it too.

Kim Kardashian is the height of American celebrity, with the power to set or signpost a trend. Only a day after she was photographed in a gown made for her by the exalted French designer Thierry Mugler, Fashion Nova began selling a replica.[1] When Kim's younger half-sister, the even more influential Kylie Jenner, threw a star-studded 21st birthday party, every dress worn and papped was cloned within hours. Fashion Nova was not just fast fashion, it was the fastest. The process of recycling, or stealing, runway designs is well known and widely practised, says Bimi. 'Celebrities wear these gorgeous gowns, they release it on social media, fast-fashion brands pick up on it, release it to the mass audience. These people wear them for about a day ... because on Instagram you can't wear anything twice.' As Bimi and I sat on the roof of the Nomad, a luxury hotel frequented by holidaying footballers, she remarked, 'I think we're in an age where people aspire to something greater, something higher, more famous, more popular, more loved, and fast fashion has allowed for that. It's allowed for people to shorten the gap between [them and] unattainable celebrities.'

Whenever Kim Kardashian posted a new fashion piece, Fashion Nova would have a version ready to go within hours. The turnaround time was so fast, many suspected the socialite and the company of working together in secret, a theory Kim denies.[2] I asked Joel, a talented marketer who worked with Fashion Nova, if he knew whether they collaborated. 'I really don't, and even if I did, I wouldn't say.' However, what he did reveal was that at one point he noticed Kim's mum and manager, Kris Jenner, conducting a meeting with Richard Saghian. So who knows what the real deal is? After all, despite Kim feuding with the brand for ripping off the Mugler dress, it was her own sister who was responsible for turning Fashion Nova into a cultural phenomenon with a single picture. In the shot, Kylie is sitting on the edge of her bed, looking over her shoulder at the camera and staring straight into the lens. She is wearing Fashion Nova jeans. The brand is tagged, and the picture has been liked almost three million times. 'That photo was viral, every tabloid picked it up,' Joel gushed.

The brand also signed up a string of B-list rappers with huge reach, including Kylie's ex-boyfriend, Tyga. Joel explains: 'They've penetrated music in a way that no one else has been able to. You've got DJ Khaled and Justin Bieber product placement bags all over the video. You've got Cardi B, the hottest artist right now, dropping Fashion Nova's name left and right. You've got the Kardashians!'

All of this paid off. In 2021, Fashion Nova surpassed 20 million Instagram followers. Three years earlier, it had become the internet's most googled fashion brand, and the company posted revenues of $294m.[3] Fashion Nova invites aspiring influencers to buy and model its clothes, then tag their photos @fashionnova and #NovaBabe. Over 10 million posts to date have been made by ordinary young women auditioning to get the brand's attention. Each is hoping to become a paid NovaBabe, an ambassador who receives gifted clothes, the Instagram equivalent of being on the VIP table.

Fashion Nova's website: *Wannabe a #NovaBabe? Do you have what it takes to be a #NovaBabe? Are you the OOTD [outfit of the day] queen who can literally rock anything?! Do you have your own style that is admired by others?? If that's you, we want you to join our #NovaSquad!*

Many aspiring influencers pay for hauls of Fashion Nova clothes to review and model, viewing it as an investment in what they hope will become a job. In reality, they're providing the company with free labour as promo girls, giving the brand edited adverts they did not have to pay for. The small number of women the company actually hand-picks for free clothes all have a similar aesthetic. They are young, with narrow waists, wide hips and thick lips. They have hourglass figures and wear clothing that clings to their skin: an aesthetic known as 'Insta baddie'. If these women are black, they looked mixed-race or light-skinned, and if they're white, they have dark hair and bronzed skin. They fit the casting call for a Kanye West video and look like they share cosmetic surgeons with the Kardashians.

Today, Bimi runs a boutique branding firm that recruits models and provides marketing content for new fashion labels trying to replicate Fashion Nova's success. I ask her how the brands choose their models. 'They base it on the look that's trending right now: the Kardashian look,' she replies. 'It's very curvaceous, mostly racially ambiguous.' Bimi, a beautiful dark woman, said that one of her clients only wanted to work with light-skinned models: 'Every time they would cast a model, that's the aesthetic that they would cast.'

A new wave of pop-up talent agencies like the London-based Above and Beyond Group swipe through social media to scout for models and influencers who match this lucrative brief. Their roster looks diverse, but although most are not white, there is a homogeneity of ambiguous beige and light brown. As Bimi remarks, 'In the nineties, straight long blonde hair and huge boobs and a real thin body was in. I think every age has its trending look.'

Fashion Nova may not have created this trend, but it has reinforced it. Fast-fashion companies throw vast amounts of money and products at the young women they pick to wear their clothes, and they have created a new economy that appears to offer easy jobs to the prettiest girls on the internet. Beauty has always been a commodity, but now it is far easier for women to monetise it themselves – if they have the right look. The belief among many young women that being desirable pays has led them to not only surgically change their shape but in some cases to even fake their ethnicity.

A black fish that is not black

At the age of 19, Aga began noticing that the pictures she took of herself and posted online were getting more and more attention. 'I didn't really have an approach. If I went out and I liked how I looked, I would take a picture.' The grid on her Instagram page has an all-too-familiar grammar. Aga is full length, and her outfit of the day – whether fitted jeans with a crop top, a jumpsuit or a patterned polyester dress – hugs her full hourglass figure. Underneath she writes a playful caption such as *A daily dose of your thickums.* Her skin is a light caramel brown and her hair is dark. Most of the selfies are taken in front of her bedroom mirror. Aga told me she had no desire to be internet-famous, but popular theme pages celebrating curvaceous women found her pictures and reposted them, sending them relatively viral. One post was viewed over 147,000 times, and soon thousands of men began following her. Aga became a local pin-up. 'I think nowadays people just love thick [curvy] girls,' she says.

Aga's pictures also caught the attention of fast-fashion companies and brands investing heavily in influencer marketing. It was then she started to think, 'Let me try and make more out of this.' The east Londoner was studying accounting, but saw providing promo as a potential side hustle. She turned her Instagram page into a business account that gives users metrics about who is watching their page, and then began tagging fashion brands including Fashion Nova. Not long after, they started gifting her clothes and so did their arch rival Pretty Little Thing. Aga had the desired aesthetic and the right audience. She also began working as an affiliate for Protein World, a supplements company, who gave her a discount code to promote to her followers. She got paid a commission for everybody who used her code on purchases.

'Most of the time brands don't actually pay me, they just give me clothes. They're like here, here's the clothes, do whatever you want with them as long as you tag us.' When I interviewed Aga in 2019, she had 50,000 followers. Months later she surpassed 250,000. At the time of writing, most of the money she makes online is from ads and affiliate work for local companies. She became one of a dozen ambassadors for a London-based chauffeur company targeting those in the inner city desperate to present themselves as successful. The company regularly recruits attractive young women with significant numbers of followers to act as digital promo girls for their large male audience. Each ambassador generates an income from the people who use their discount code. The ambassadors have a uniform aesthetic. Once again, they appear black but light brown or mixed heritage and ethnically ambiguous. Aga fitted in.

In September 2018, the teenager photographed herself in an outfit composed of items she had been given to promote: clothes, phone case, eyelashes, and even hair, which came courtesy of a small Afro hair store based in the East Midlands. In the picture, she is standing in her trademark pose. Her hips are wide and her waist is so narrow it looks like an optical illusion. Her skin is brown, her lips are full and her wavy black hair is in cornrow braids, a popular Afro hairstyle. She is the picture of a confident and beautiful young black woman. The only problem is, Aga is not a black woman at all. She was born in Poland and would become one of the many white influencers accused of 'blackfishing'.

In November 2018, a young writer named Wanna Thompson fired the first shot and defined the term with the viral tweet: 'Can we start a thread of all the white girls cosplaying as black women on Instagram?' The internet exploded. Aga ritually scrolls through Twitter, Instagram and Snapchat the way previous generations used to read the morning paper. 'I woke up,' she says, 'and went on Twitter, and I'm going through the threads when I saw an interesting one. I scroll and randomly see my picture!' The next thing she knew, her phone was buzzing with messages from friends and strangers to let her know the world was talking about her.

A list was shared thousands of times with the before-and-after pictures of young white women between the ages of 17 and 21 who had transformed themselves from having pale skin, straight hair and narrow features into having brown skin, full lips and wavy hair with the help of dark make-up, contouring and even wigs. There are even YouTube videos showing you how to do it. Emma Hallberg, a Fashion Nova ambassador with dark brown skin, had built up a loyal base of over 300,000 followers who believed she was of mixed heritage and who followed her for beauty tips. When she was included in the list, her stunned followers messaged her to ask if it was true. Could she really be white? Emma replied that she had never claimed to be anything else, despite painting her face brown. Some of her followers tweeted that they felt deceived.

For Aga, the controversy led to her Instagram page hitting almost 1.5 million impressions. She was accused of pretending to be black, of racism, and even minstrelsy, referring to the old performance where white entertainers darkened their skin to mimic and mock black people. Newspapers and academics across the world were perplexed, but the phenomenon was not difficult to understand. Even the Kardashians have transformed the way they look. Kylie Jenner's cosmetic procedures made her appear ethnically mixed or 'exotic'. Kim Kardashian was accused of blackfishing when she appeared on the cover of the magazine *7 Hollywood* with brown skin in the guise of African-American Motown legend Diana Ross. 'I did understand where people were coming from,' said Aga. 'I'm a millennial. I am on social media. I see the trends and stuff like that, it's not like I looked at my picture and thought they're making up things from thin air, but what can I do about that?' I asked if she planned to stop wearing Afro hairstyles; she said it was too much of a 'sensitive conversation' and she had not made up her mind.

Aga was born in the Polish city Krakow but grew up in Barking, in east London, one of the most diverse districts in Europe. The on- and offline world she lives in is no longer gripped by a beauty standard that has white women on top. For Aga, the aspirational face of beauty belongs to Teyana Taylor, the chiselled chestnut R&B singer who was the centrepiece of Kanye West's *Flashdance*-inspired music video 'Fade'. Taylor has been an ambassador for both Fashion Nova and its rival Pretty Little Thing. 'Teyana Taylor has a beautiful body, she is absolutely beautiful,' Aga says admiringly.

Aga is part of a generation that has only known a world where the internet is supreme and the most dominant aesthetic in youth culture is hip-hop. The genre's music and fashion dictate not only what and who is desirable but also the part you can play in its billion-dollar industries and the clothing companies attaching themselves to it for clout. To be shapeless and pale with narrow European features has little currency in the part of the internet where a Fashion Nova ambassador gig makes you a VIP. Today, many young white women in their teens and early twenties are conforming to this standard by contouring, and their racial transformation has an economic incentive too: this cosplay actually pays.

The ethics and politics of beauty trends are rarely discussed in a world where influencers happily sell their following to the highest bidder. One BBC investigation found that a trio of high-profile influencers appeared happy to promote a diet drink laced with cyanide. The drink did not really exist, but the influencers thought it did. When confronted, they claimed they were just doing their job. There is a notable abdication of responsibility by many influencers when it comes to the brands they are paid to not only promote but often reinvent. This is especially so in the case of fast fashion, and particularly Fashion Nova. Nevertheless, it is with the brands deploying exploitative models that the greater responsibility lies.

Fast money

Fashion Nova has a simple model: it buys cheaply manufactured clothes made for a pittance and manages to glamorise them enough to sell them for a substantial profit. It would almost certainly not be the juggernaut success it is without the stardust of influencers. Its clothes are the epitome of plastic masquerading as platinum. The brand captures all the contradictions of California, where its clothes are presented on the bodies of LA's finest but manufactured in the city's hidden sweatshops.

To foreigners, the Los Angeles fashion district may conjure up images of celebrity and hipster fashionistas, but in reality, the 90-block neighbourhood is anything but stylish. It is an industrial site made up of warehouses, wholesalers and fly-by-night sweatshops operating in one of the most corrosive sectors on earth. The global garment industry is the world's third largest manufacturing industry after automobiles and tech, and is a bigger contributor to climate change than international aviation and shipping combined. It consumes lake-sized volumes of fresh water each year, and in the process gives off huge levels of chemical and plastic pollution.

Scattered across downtown LA, an estimated 3,000 small factories employ Latina migrants to meet the demand fuelled by brands like Fashion Nova. Yet over 300,000 tons of the clothes produced end up in household bins each year, with less than 1 per cent recycled.[4] If the environmental concerns are not alarming enough, the industry also has a chronic problem with labour exploitation. In Western economies, undocumented migrants are being paid poverty wages in makeshift factories from Leicester to Los Angeles, while turning around the must-have celebrity dress of the day before tomorrow's new flavour arrives. Influencers dress up to market these clothes under the banner of self-expression, but the workers manufacturing them have little voice.

In the LA fashion district, an estimated 50,000 garment workers toiling on factory floors are supported by just one advocacy group helping them to receive fair pay. The Garment Worker Center operates out of a tiny office in a multistorey building mostly comprised of textile wholesalers.

The walls inside are grey, with a blue tint. A maze of corridors eventually leads to a wooden door with a reminder of the fear most garment workers constantly live under. A sign reads: 'This is a private organisation. We do not give you permission to enter this office based on our 4th amendment rights under the United States constitution. Unless you have a warrant, we do not wish to speak with you, answer your questions, sign or hand you documents based on our 5th amendment rights.' The message is for the Immigration and Customs Enforcement agency, otherwise known as ICE. In LA, the vast majority of garment workers are from Mexico and Central America. Many are undocumented monolingual Spanish speakers.

Virginia, a mother of four, is in the United States without permission. The 45-year-old Latina recounts her life to me through an interpreter. She was born in Guatemala, where her daughters remain stranded, while she, her partner and her eldest sons live in America, unable to travel back due to their immigration status. 'I don't have any papers. I'm not documented and I came across the border. I came by myself and followed my husband here. It was very hard. I had to walk for two days and two nights in the middle of the desert,' she tells me.

When she left Guatemala, the economy was bad, but 20 years on, the country also has one of the highest murder rates in the world, the third highest rate of female murder and a huge exodus of civilians in search of safety. 'If I could, I'd bring my daughters over here,' she says. Her voice cracks and her eyes begin to flood. She describes how one of her daughters was raped and her brother was murdered. Despite earning a pittance as a factory checker, Virginia is her family's main breadwinner. Yet she is barely making enough to cover the rent, despite regularly sending money south of the border. She has been in the garment trade for 17 years and has spent her working life moving from factory to factory: when the work dries up at one place, she will walk around the fashion district until she finds another. 'Last week I was working at a factory on Stamford and Pico Boulevard,' she says, but she was told by management that there was no more work for her and that they would call when things picked up. When she went to collect her wages, she noticed a discrepancy. Not for the first time, she had been unlawfully underpaid.

According to the director of the Garment Worker Center, Marissa, there is an 85 per cent rate of wage theft in the industry. 'That means 85 per cent of the factories are paying under the minimum wage. Through our casework we've seen an average of $5.50 an hour.' The minimum wage in California is $13.25 an hour. Undocumented workers are easy to exploit, not just because they are willing to work for less but because they are too scared to mount wage disputes for fear of reprisals that could see them deported. The indignity is that Virginia is being robbed by an employer making clothes for fast-fashion companies that are worth hundreds of millions of dollars.

Virginia's worst memories are from a rat-infested sweat-shop on 22nd Street, between Main and Broadway, south of the fashion district. 'I suffered a lot in that factory. I would even get rat urine on me sometimes. There was like rat poop on the ground. There were rats walking along the ceiling, their droppings would fall on us,' she says. 'I think that with Fashion Nova, when people buy their products they probably think the items are made in a very clean place, but actually the clothing that they're buying, rats have probably peed on it.'

Marissa tells me that the Garment Worker Center has helped workers get back over $6m in unpaid wages, and estimates that that amounts to $30,000–50,000 per worker once damages are included. The trouble is that companies regularly disappear before facing justice. Most factories consist of only a handful of people, which means it's easy for them to shut down and vanish. When a wage dispute opens up, 'they can close down literally overnight' and the law allows their clients, the fast-fashion companies, to claim deniability of any wage theft or unlawful practice. 'They're well aware that it's padding their profit margin [and from] that point of view they're definitely responsible,' she says.

At the heart of the fast-fashion industry is an unsustainable model of hyper-production and consumption. It is forecast that by 2030, global clothing consumption will rise by 63 per cent, from 62 million tons today to 102 million tons.[5] That is equivalent to an extra 500 billion T-shirts floating around the planet, more than 70 times the number of people. Fast fashion has even become a challenge for international diplomacy.[6] According to the UN, the equivalent of almost three planets would be required to provide the natural resources needed to sustain current lifestyles given the projected growth in global population by 2050. The world's biggest fast-fashion brands remain ASOS, H&M, Boohoo and Pretty Little Thing, but Marissa and the Garment Worker Center have noticed one company popping up again and again in complaints from garment workers. Overnight, Fashion Nova appears to be the fastest-growing fast-fashion company that sweatshops are fighting to win contracts with.

Fashion Nova did not invent the fast-fashion model, but they appear to be better than any of their competitors at driving the demand for clothes manufactured to be worn just once, by turning a generation of young women into mass marketers without a care for what they are selling. 'Their model is built on creating the demand,' says Marissa. 'I feel like it is not even that someone like Fashion Nova is lying about who they are. They are actually creating [an] environment [where] people don't care.' In Fashion Nova's flagship store in Panorama City Mall, the clothes on sale profit from messages of female empowerment. The brand promises that women can be as successful as NovaBabes like Cardi B. The rapper's own fashion line sold out within hours. In the store, colourful tops proudly sport the slogans 'Equality' and 'Independent Woman', and yet Fashion Nova is a company owned and run by a man accused of profiting from clothes kept cheap by the exploitation of vulnerable women in his supply chain.

The quality of the clothes can be so poor that some fashion bloggers have even accused the company of being scammers. However, none of this has stopped its boom in sales, or the queues of young women desperate for a Fashion Nova brand deal, or even just some free clothes. When it comes down to it, the company's success is as a manufacturer of hype rather than clothing. However, the impact of fast fashion and the Kardashian look has had unexpected consequences elsewhere: an entire economy has sprung up to achieve the signature NovaBabe aesthetic, with surgical procedures marketed by companies even more ruthless than Fashion Nova itself.

2

UNDER THE KNIFE

Micro-influencer Cherrise Massey may not be a celebrity, but she is working on it. In a Manchester hotel suite notoriously booked by adult entertainers for porn shoots, the 23-year-old asks me if I'd like to see her breast. 'Sure,' I say. Weeks earlier, towards the tail end of Britain's first COVID lockdown, the young mother of two boarded a flight to Istanbul to have a breast and butt enhancement operation that she hoped would take her closer to her desired look, but as we speak post-op, her breast has a gaping wound where a nipple should be. 'Tomorrow I could wake up and half of the boob can be black and fall off,' she says matter-of-factly. 'It's scary, it doesn't smell good. It's rotten flesh.'

Cherrise is of medium height, with light brown skin and a long black weave. Her face and teeth look as if they have been edited by an Instagram filter, and in reality, they have. 'Last year Instagram had a few filters that chisel your nose, jaw and fill the lips. I went to the girl who does my filler and I said I want it so my face is like the filter so I don't have to use the filter. Now when I use the filter it does not change my face.' She is beaming with pride. Since she was 18, she has gone under the knife as regularly as on her summer holidays. She has had full-body lipo, implants, veneers and the infamous Brazilian butt lift (BBL), which transfers fat from unflattering areas such as the waist or stomach and pumps them into the behind to inflate it like a balloon. The procedure, which was made famous by Kim Kardashian, has the highest death rate of any cosmetic surgery.[1]

In the influencer economy, how you look is a currency, albeit one increasingly set by algorithms and editing apps. The rising and real rewards of accruing followers drawn by desirable photographs are pushing more young adults – especially women – under the knife to achieve the aesthetic that will help them trend. 'I want the curves, the hourglass figure, the Kardashian figure. I want the big bum, I want the boobs,' Cherrise says. 'If I had that desired look and that desired body, it's clothing brands, it's gym brands that want to collab with you, it's a financial pathway. I said it to my parents [and] they said "Why are you getting all this surgery?" and I said "I'm investing in my future" and they couldn't understand.'

Those who do understand now see young women like Cherrise as an easy meal for the taking. There is a fast-growing industry of pop-up companies in under-regulated countries like Turkey selling cosmetic procedures over Instagram. They appear overnight and hire freelance surgeons to carry out procedures on patients from more affluent economies. At best, the surgeries they offer girls from western Europe are more affordable than procedures in their home countries, but at worst, the companies can leave patients in danger by hiring dubious doctors whilst being unable to provide aftercare if things go wrong. The risks are heavily filtered. Despite advertising guidelines for cosmetic surgeries being strict in the UK, the main regulator cannot take action against companies operating abroad, as they are out of their jurisdiction.

The company Cherrise found operating in Istanbul was endorsed by numerous glamorous Instagram models, including several she knew. Avrupamed is one of the many enterprises that target aspiring influencers as both customers and potential salespeople. The company has a busy pipeline of predominantly young women from Britain, Sweden, France and Germany who move in and out at speed and are often unaware who their surgeon is going to be. Its booming Instagram page is littered with the before-and-after pictures of young bodies laid out on operating tables like carcasses in a butcher's shop window. At the last count, it had gained over 60,000 followers. Cherrise told me the company offered her aggressive discounts because of her small but significant social media following of young women just like her.

The day of Cherrise's consultation in Istanbul was the same day she was operated on. This turnaround would be unthinkable in the US or the UK for a planned surgery. Her procedure was also botched. Breast implants were used as bum implants and were subsequently rejected by her body, and that was not all. The surgery lasted nine hours and her blood levels dropped to dangerously low levels. Afterwards, she bled heavily but she was discharged after only four days. When she returned to the UK, her health deteriorated so rapidly that she was hospitalised, and she was told the actions of the clinic in Istanbul had led to her developing necrosis. Her breast was rotting due to a severe infection from an untreated blood clot.

When I made contact with the company to hear their side of the story, the spokesman was haughty and aggressive. They accused Cherrise of being desperate for attention. A notable lack of concern shone through their reply, which was strewn with spelling errors. Cherrise 'just wants money', they said, as if I had not seen with my own eyes the pus pouring from her breast. I spoke to another woman in her forties who corroborated the company's disdain for the women paying them. She herself was diagnosed with broken ribs after a suspected emergency CPR during her surgery in Istanbul. Her NHS doctor concluded that she had most likely died and been resuscitated on the operating table.[2] If so, it was an event Avrupamed failed to tell her about afterwards.

Indecent proposal

YouTuber Nella Rose is an unusual NovaBabe. Unlike many of the company's roster of Instagram models, 22-year-old Nella has grown a cult following through her charisma. She began posting videos from her university halls. Her quirky take on sex, diets and gossip has been a hit with a generation of urbanite black British college girls. The young women who have subscribed in large numbers have laughed and cried with her as she came of age in a melting pot of black cultures. They listened to West African Afrobeat, African-American hip-hop, Caribbean dancehall, and the new Afroswing that blended all three while adding a London accent. These young educated women are big consumers of online content, but in the past they have rarely been represented or catered for on mainstream TV. On YouTube they have found a voice, and personalities like Nella play the role of relatable big sister and confidante. She says what is on her mind, flexes her confidence and shares her woes. In many of her videos she speaks jovially about her struggles with body confidence.

She has a reassuring average build that is part of her appeal with young women under the burden of impossible beauty standards.

Nella may not be Kim Kardashian famous, but the devotion of her viewers makes her attractive to brands desperate to capture the attention of young women just like her. The diet supplements company Protein World sponsors her videos on how to lose weight, and Fashion Nova pays her to promote clothes from their plus-sized range. Nella films herself trying on Fashion Nova's wacky items and posts the images on both Instagram and YouTube. After every post, her comments section lights up with applause. Her inbox is full of messages of support and approaches from other companies. One of the most disturbing came after Nella posted a picture of herself wearing a figure-hugging black dress from Fashion Nova: 'The dress on the last post would look even more amazing on you after our BBL treatment! Don't you think the same?' This direct message was from an infamous cosmetic surgery called Clinichub.

Just like Avrupamed, Clinichub is a fast-growing company that could only exist in the social media age. It was founded by the serial entrepreneur Ibrahim Kuzu, a prolific Turkish salesman living in London who has launched 10 companies in just over a decade. Before incorporating Clinichub, the 40-year-old had founded and dissolved a restaurant, a car company and an investment firm. However, it was young women's growing desperation to be desirable online that has changed his life.

Where Kuzu has been most successful is in aggressively tapping into the niche corner of female black British lifestyle influencers. He offers them free procedures, courtesy of the freelance Turkish surgeons he hires, if they promote Clinichub and attribute their new-found body confidence to their remodelled shape. Some even claim to have been paid for procedures. Kuzu incentivises micro-influencers to post positive reviews about dangerous surgeries and recommend them as a method of self-improvement that more and more young women have gravitated towards.

One girl I managed to speak to, and followed for over a year, is 20-year-old Jade. The north Londoner grew up with an awareness of how she looked. At six feet two, she has bright green eyes, curly hair and a face that has turned heads since she was a teenager. When she was 15 years old, she accidentally built a following of 15,000 by posting pictures of herself. The account was hacked and she has been trying to rebuild the following ever since. 'Knowing what I know now, I could have made a lot of money off that page which is quite frustrating,' she says. Her life has parallels with Cherrise's. Jade was born into a mixed-heritage working-class family in the unfashionable suburbs of north London and left school at 16 for the world of work while her friends headed to college. 'My mum was working just to pay the bills. I didn't really see pocket money, so as soon as I left secondary school she wanted me to get an apprenticeship to help her with extra income.'

The problem is that modern apprenticeships barely pay and rarely lead to job progression, despite being hailed by British politicians as a way to earn and learn. In many cases companies have used apprenticeship schemes to legally pay youngsters beneath the minimum wage whilst saddling them with heavy workloads. Jade picked up work at a small cleaning company with half a dozen staff where she did tasks outside her job role and worked extra hours for no overtime. She eventually left, but without any qualifications she wondered what she could do next. At 20 years old, she found herself a mother of two, unemployed, unpartnered and concerned about her job prospects.

'I'd love to go back to school. I don't know what I'd study. I just feel like without A levels, without a degree, you kind of put yourself in a bracket with the kind of jobs you can get, what kind of income you can get, where you can really excel … A lot of people do break out of it. However, it's very hard and you kind of need to know the right people … I'd need to wait another five years until the boys are in primary school until I can consider part-time university, but even then I'd need to go and do A levels just to get in.'

Barely out of her teenage years, Jade was trapped between the burden of parenthood and the promise of youth. The career that caught her eye was capturing attention online as a YouTuber or Instagrammer: 'There is a lot of money to be made and if I can do that at home whilst taking care of my boys then I will take every opportunity I can to do so,' she said.

She relished the potential paid opportunities to promote the clothes of internet fast-fashion brands. 'The main ones, Pretty Little Thing, Boohoo, Fashion Nova … they have a very specific look, the vixen look, [for] which a lot of girls go to the Dominican Republic for surgery.' She downloaded photo editing apps that showed her what she would look like if she narrowed her waist, enlarged her bottom and broadened her natural physique. She was born with a straight and athletic body, but the more time she spent online, the more she wanted to transform her figure, in the hope that it could help her gain influencer work.

While scrolling across the social media pages of girls who had had BBLs, Jade came across the YouTube page of a controversial micro-influencer with the stage name Renee R Fabulous. Renee is boisterous, loud and dramatic. She had packed in her low-paid job as a hotel chambermaid once she had grown her page spinning elaborate yarns about dating sugar daddies, generating verbal and even physical beef with rival influencers. The wahala would become fodder for the urban gossip blogosphere, and led to a gig as a paid ambassador for Fashion Nova Curve.

Her videos were like a DIY version of reality show *Love & Hip Hop*, with Renee inventing drama and boasting about 'securing the bag' (making money).

Renee had completely changed her shape and posted supposedly candid videos with titles like 'The truth about my BBL, very detailed, everything you need to know'. In the video she recommends Clinichub to the thousands of viewers who have watched it. Nowhere in the video does she declare that she is an ambassador for the company, with a deal where she receives discounts and free surgeries for drawing in young clients. One of the many women to find out about Clinichub through Renee was Jade.

Botched

One of the more bizarre aspects of the boom in surgery culture is the cult of young women setting up anonymous pages that display their obsession with famous cosmetic surgeons and transforming their bodies. On these pages, teenage girls and adult women religiously follow the Instagram models they want to look like, repost pictures of these models, and forward them to surgeons asking if they can remodel them in the image of their body inspirations. The women call themselves the 'dolls' of the surgeries and surgeons they lionise. Clinichub's most prominent surgeon, Furkan Certel, has a following of over 35,000. Some of the names these women go by include @ clinichub.babe, @clinhub_dollx and @Furkansdoll. Such accounts do not identify their real names, but one of them we have already met: Jade.

In May 2019, Jade became one of Clinichub's clients. 'I had 360 lip and a BBL. So I only had my waist, my stomach, my back liposuctioned and mainly reinjected into my hips.' The Brazilian butt lift is an extensive procedure with a significant rate of fatality or post-op disfigurement. Physical recovery time is up to six months and the mental strain can last even longer. Jade had opted for a tamer version, dubbed the light BBL. The procedure sculpted hips into her straight figure and boosted her buttocks, but was more subtle than the extreme forms that make a body look wildly disproportionate by adding a bum to a figure with tiny thighs.

Jade captured the recovery process on her Instagram page and told followers to subscribe to the new YouTube channel she had set up. The images she posted showed a changed body still in its early days. It regularly swelled, and because the surgery sculpted newly transferred fat, she could not yet do simple tasks, as she had to constantly wear a post-op compression bodysuit. She missed being able to sit on her ass and avoided playing with her children. Her body felt stiff, but nevertheless she was initially happy. 'I've got the typical Instabody,' she posted with a smiley emoji face.

While in Turkey, she had thanked Clinichub for giving her life a new trajectory. 'I came here looking like a fridge and I'm leaving looking like Kylie Jenner.'

However, there was pain to Jade's pleasure. The procedure left her itchy, constipated and on an emotional rollercoaster. 'Sometimes because of the swelling I feel like "what have I done to myself?" which can heighten my anxiety to the point where I don't even want to go to the supermarket … Yesterday I had my toddler run into my hip where he's left a small dent. I don't know if only I can see it or maybe I'm just paranoid.'

Jade shared some of the more minor mental toils in the community of dolls. It was common for the girls to caption the date they had booked their surgery for in the hope of finding a buddy who would be heading out to Turkey at the same time with the same surgeon. Afterwards, they shared pictures of the results and the process seemed both cathartic and sisterly. On the surface, the dolls' community appeared to be a safe place where women could find out the truth about drastic procedures from their peers. However, in practice there was an unspoken code of omission and dishonesty.

Unknown to their impressionable audience, Clinichub had been botching surgeries, and the dolls who were sitting offline with unsatisfactory results were saying the opposite online. Uncertainty is part of medicine, but risk is amplified when an often unattainable ideal is being pursued via such drastic means. In the community of dolls, young women were refusing to be honest with their followers and were arguably misleading their friends.

Aspiring YouTuber Fleur was back home in London when, weeks after a BBL, her fat-enhanced backside began to leak. The injected fat was being rejected by her body and rotting through the pores of her skin. The outcome is not uncommon for a procedure that requires a body to comply with a store of fat that is not supposed to be there. The consequence for Fleur was a crater the size of her fist in her butt. To make matters worse, she told me she had caught an infection from the procedure and was now hospitalised. Nevertheless, on her Instagram she still presented a picture of happiness and did not immediately warn the doll community of the downsides she had experienced.

Something similar happened to Clinichub ambassador Renee. She had a second BBL with the company, and soon pictures of her post-operative behind appeared, revealing a severely disproportionate body shape. At first she concealed the extent of the damage, but eventually, when the pictures went viral, she admitted that the surgery had jeopardised her health. In January 2021, she spoke publicly about having three botched procedures with the company and apologised to her followers, saying, 'To anybody that I've influenced to go and get surgery, I want to literally say I'm absolutely so sorry.'[3]

Like Cherrise, another 'doll' had her nipples fall off after a breast enhancement by Clinichub left a gaping wound. The picture is as gruesome as it sounds. A third young woman in the community, a nursing student from Coventry named Latice, told me that a BBL with Clinichub left her burned and disfigured, with one hip curved and the other flat. She suffered from post-surgery depression and then had a full mental breakdown.

What was significant was that none of the women dared share their ordeal publicly. 'I'm not being honest, I'm not happy,' Latice told me, 'but I haven't disclosed it.' She didn't have the money to pay for a second procedure, so was staying silent in the hope that Clinichub would correct it for free. The same was true for Fleur. Latice said she knew of other botched jobs that were not being publicly declared for fear of embarrassment and in the hope of further corrective work. Some women even aspired to be made ambassadors. In her view nobody was being honest about the true risks involved. In the past, awareness of the dangers had been a check on demand, but against the spirit of the guidelines set by the Advertising Standards Authority, micro-influencers make modern surgery look mundane, ordinary and risk-free.

Filtered

When I met Ibrahim Kuzu at the offices of Channel 4 News, where I work, business was booming. With bookings lined up for the next six months, he was in a buoyant mood. Five minutes after meeting me, he had forensically searched my body with his eyes, looking for any flaw or insecurity he could find. I was trying to convince him to let me observe his operation, and he was trying to convince me to be one of his male models, even offering me a procedure for free in return: penis enlargement, new hairline, man-boob removal, anything. He felt that if more men went on social media to break the taboo about surgery, that might help to boost sales. I was given a brief glimpse of the intensity that drove his company. He relentlessly encouraged me to get surgery to improve myself and told me it would help increase my followers on Instagram. As someone over 30 who is reasonably secure about their looks, I dreaded to think how his hard sell might impact on impressionable young people in their late teens and early twenties.

If salesmen like Ibrahim are pushy, at least his approach is obvious. But what his company – and many other pop-up cosmetic surgery companies – have learnt is that it is more effective to delegate the business development to micro-influencers like Cherrise: those with a following of around 10,000, and often even considerably fewer. They may have a modest community, but the young women who consume their content do not realise they are saleswomen in disguise.

Twenty-six-year-old Yasmin became an ambassador for one of Clinichub's competitors, Spectra. The young woman from east London tells me that cosmetic surgery changed her life, and is incredibly open about the number of procedures she has had since turning 21. 'I've done two liposuctions. I've done two fat transfers including a BBL. I've done a breast augmentation ... breast implants. The areas I've done liposuction have been my stomach, my arms, my stomach.' She pauses. 'I've done liposuction God knows how many times and I've just had my lips done!' Whenever her body expanded further than she liked, she made an appointment with her doctor.

Yasmin had struggled with her sense of self even before the ubiquity of Instagram. She had left home in her mid teens, lived in a hostel and had a turbulent relationship that ended after her boyfriend was unfaithful. 'I definitely hated my body. I was on antidepressants at one point in my life. I think my relationship wasn't helping me either. I felt really ugly in the relationship. I felt that I wasn't good enough. I remember in uni two girls walked past me and they were probably at most a size 10 and I burst into tears. I called my friend and she was like what's wrong? I was like everyone's so skinny. I was having a breakdown.'

Yasmin used her student loan to get her first procedure and began posting videos on Snapchat. 'I was snapping in the hospital practically with no clothes on and that got my views up a lot, so from there I started trying to build on my other socials, Instagram and Twitter. I also said I'm gonna do YouTube.' She set up a YouTube channel, 'Yasmin Pinkk', with a public persona in the same mould as A-list rapper Nicki Minaj on her debut studio album, *Pink Friday*. The rapper herself has had multiple procedures and was one of the earliest exponents of the BBL shape that Yasmin built her page around.

By the standards of YouTube fame, Yasmin's channel, which is dedicated to talking about her procedures, is microscopic. She has fewer than 1,000 subscribers and her most popular video has just under 8,000 views, but those watching are exactly the kind of young women that companies like Clinichub, Avrupamed and Spectra are trying to attract, and often girls like Yasmin are their most effective way to recruit. 'I never knew the amount of girls that wanted to do surgery two years ago,' Yasmin says. 'They just needed a few people [to encourage them] and I'm not talking about the [big] influencers.'

As Yasmin sees it, nobody trusts big influencers; it's the smaller micro-influencers like her who are seen as more relatable, trustworthy and therefore commercially valuable. Her videos single-handedly elevated Spectra's profile among her audience of young black British women. 'They needed someone that was just like them. An average girl that's not famous, hasn't got this clout. They needed a regular girl to talk about it.' So Yasmin did, and in return she has been a lucrative ambassador for her Turkish cosmetic surgeon.

'When I took it to YouTube and they saw the impact that it had, we started having talks about what can I do to help.' She talks about the new financial arrangement as if it's charity. On her YouTube channel is the written notice 'My doctor has permitted me to give any of my viewers his contact details, if interested, so hit me up on one of my socials. Let's make this happen!' However, her relationship with Spectra is far more official than this, and she even claims there was a contract for her to sign. 'For me to do this, obviously I'm getting freebies. That alone is enough. I got my lips done, they didn't charge me for that. I never pay for travel. I don't pay for medication, my hospital stay, they let me stay there for free!'

The benefit to the company is clear. Yasmin estimates that in 2019 she spoke directly to 30 girls on Spectra's behalf, and this doesn't include the handful of her own friends who have since had procedures there. 'People who did not know how to contact my doctor [before] have come through me to make a consultation. I've even gone as far as setting up consultations. They've asked me questions that I don't need to contact my doctor for – especially on surgeries that I've already done.'

The incentives the company give Yasmin have created a conflict of interest that is not clear to those who watch her parade of procedures. Her followers are unlikely to find out about any risks or downsides. Instead, she shouts from the rooftops about her new confidence and the paid opportunities she receives from having a figure like a Coca-Cola bottle. 'If I look at brands like Fashion Nova or Pretty Little Thing, not trying to be funny but have you seen the models that they use! You're looking at them like "there's no way that is gonna look like that on me" so it has you really thinking. You also notice these companies give out a lot of freebies to these girls that look like that and these girls, that's how their Instagram profiles have grown. I know this because I've only been trying to build my Instagram page for the last year and I've seen the impact it's [her BBL] had … Just this week alone the number of invitations I've had to do this or do that, "I'll do your eyelashes for free". It's crazy, everything comes down to social media.'

Yasmin's surgery initiated her into a world of brand ambassador deals and attention. 'My social media has grown. I've joined podcasts, interviews. My YouTube has grown. I'm being acknowledged,' she says gratefully. It is this economy, she suggests, that is driving surgery tourism. However, despite being a convert herself, even Yasmin is nervous about filtering technology, which deluges us with pictures of other people's unattainable looks. The girls contacting her are getting younger and younger.

'It's mainly social media, all these editing apps, it's all these Instamodels. That is what is causing these problems, especially the girls in America. This surgery that we're doing has always been a trend but it was never a trend in the UK, this was only a trend in America. It's very easy to get your body done in America, even illegally with you know butt injections, butt implants, you name it. Something happened and Instagram has obviously taken over a lot [from] Facebook … That's where these girls are picking these ideas from.' What Yasmin does not seem to appreciate is that she herself is one of 'these girls'. In fact even worse than that, she is actively setting up consultations for her own remuneration.

The internet was supposed to democratise the spread of information and make companies more open by elevating the independent voice of consumers, but the world of surgery is just one example of how easily that can be corrupted by warped incentive models. Several months after first interviewing Jade, I got back in touch with her. I had been following her life online and a lot had changed. Now aged 21, she had split with her partner and had paid off the cost of her surgery through selling twerk videos on OnlyFans. She was also booking modelling jobs thanks to her new figure and was even considering additional bum implants. But she no longer wanted to talk because she was unsure how she felt about surgery, or at least that was what she told me. The truth is that Jade was still an impressionable young woman still creating herself.

Teenagers and young adults everywhere on the planet are growing up under the unbearable pressure of being both hyper-visible to strangers and distanced from real-life friends. This became even more acute during the COVID pandemic. The young women in the doll community live in a world where the judgement of their peers is more intense than at any moment in contemporary history. On social media there is no escape from the gaze of others, even while alone. According to the famous words of the existential philosopher Sartre, hell is other people. In the social media age, that hell is closer, more prolific and more powerful than ever.

The whole system has a tragic absurdity. The dolls I spoke to have taken risks with their own bodies for the dubious reward of advertising cheaply manufactured knock-offs sewn together by exploited labourers. If Kim Kardashian made the BBL aesthetic mainstream, then fast fashion made it an aspirational career move that actually paid, and cosmetic surgery companies created an incentive model that presented invasive procedures as risk-free and necessary for aspiring influencers. It is unsurprising that the number of procedures has now soared.

When Clinichub directly messaged the influencer Nella Rose offering her a BBL to improve her shape and better present the clothes she was promoting, Nella was distraught. She took an image of the message and posted it online to shame them. The company was booed on the blogs and meme pages central to black British youth culture, even by people who had surgery appointments booked with them. Clinichub publicly apologised and gave a corporate response dripping in dishonesty. 'Clinichub pays great attention to BODY AWARENESS and BODY POSITIVITY. We believe all human bodies are perfect and we always stand for this philosophy.' If they believed this, they would not even be in business, let alone pitching up in the inboxes of young women, and they are not the only ones. Women now find themselves the targets of an entire new ecosystem of apps and platforms promising them financial freedom by selling themselves in both new and old ways.

3

FIND SOME FANS

Instagram is the perfect marketplace for sex. On Twitter and TikTok, viral users require wit. On YouTube, personality pays. Yet on Instagram, the way we look is carefully self-curated for the consumption of others. In other words, the platform thrives on lustful thirst. My friend Assed, a ripped television correspondent for Al Jazeera, can never resist posting his six-pack from his daily workouts. The platform encourages vanity and rewards the sexually desirable with big followings. As topless ab pics and booty poses have become part of Instagram's grammar, the boundary on what sex work is has shifted. If growing your social media following through selling your sex appeal is well-rewarded labour, then to many, digital sex work such as selling nudes is just another mundane hustle rather than a vice. In the years of Instagram's rise, a cultural shift has taken place: the sex worker has been recast as an aspirational hustler.

Cherrise, who we met in the last chapter, operates in that grey area between influencer work and sex work on Instagram. While trying to secure brand deals and grow her social media pages, the Manchester-based influencer also sells nude images on OnlyFans. Social-media-linked payment sites easily allow us to literally commodify ourselves and build a significant following doing so. Cam girls often have a larger following than sportsmen. The growing social cachet of this type of celebrity, along with new platforms like OnlyFans or Patreon, has made the trade more popular and diverse, less stigmatised and ever more lucrative.

Few women better personify the sky-high possibilities internet fame can bring than reality star turned megastar Belcalis Almánzar, better known as Cardi B. The former exotic dancer is the latest reincarnation of the Californian dream: a dancer who went from the strip club to the Forbes list on the strength of her unfiltered character. Cardi B's social media personality led to her being cast on the cult reality TV show *Love & Hip Hop*, but the Latina from The Bronx was not satisfied with local fame and began mapping a path to global stardom as a rapper advocating the transformational power of sex work, just in time to take advantage of the renaissance in commercialised feminism. At the heart of this movement is the questionable belief that anything that makes a woman rich is empowering for all women.

Cardi B's club anthems provide a gendered reinvention of the underdog rapper fighting their way out of the American ghetto and into a life of glamour. Her major label debut, 'Bodak Yellow', became the first single by a female rapper without another featured artist on the track to top the US *Billboard* Hot 100. The song is best captured by the standout lines 'I don't dance now, I make money moves. See I don't gotta dance I make money moves.' Her debut album, which followed 'Bodak Yellow', topped the charts and even won best rap album at the Grammys. It was hailed as a breath of fresh air, even if at its heart was the old hip-hop proverb that there is no unethical way to make money when you need it. No vice is off limits. Cash rules everything. It is unsurprising that in the post-hip-hop era, in which everything and anything is for sale, this sentiment has also become the truth of the influencer, the career of choice for Gen Z, those born after 1997, the very year Cherrise was born.

Cherrise models in low-paying rap music videos, seeks brand deals and pumps out erotic content on OnlyFans, the de facto porn platform for paid members that broadened its appeal in 2020 to host mainstream celebrities and sportsmen too. Even Cardi B has an account, where she posted behind-the-scenes videos for her duet with Megan Thee Stallion, 'WAP' (an acronym for 'wet-ass pussy'). The site, which was founded in 2016 by serial entrepreneur Tim

Stokely, allows creators to release videos and photographs to tiers of paying subscribers. Stokely himself, unlike the creators who use OnlyFans, prefers to avoid the camera and has generally opted out of attention. The secretive young entrepreneur launched the site as a way to tap into the burgeoning sexualisation of the influencer economy. Stokely's father worked in the investment arm of Barclays Bank and today is chairman of the holding group that owns the platform his son founded.

Tim Stokely had launched prior sites focused on pornographic content, but OnlyFans has brought him a whole new level of riches, with the company on track to become a unicorn. In November 2020, it had no external investors, no need for additional investment and was in profit. It claims to have paid out $2bn to creators whilst taking an unusually high commission of 20 per cent.[1] In 2020, the site had over 85 million registered users and over 450,000 content creators, with 100 making more than $1m a year.[2] Some sell raunchy but clothed pictures; others make fetish content of things like their feet; and others post full nudes. A former stripper turned contestant on the cult hit show *Love Island* reportedly made £800,000 in a single month selling access to her glamour shots. The website Patreon works in a similar way but has a wider pool of content-makers, including artists, writers and activists selling their musings and even tweets.

Sex work has always been a broad category that includes everything from escorting and stripping to cam work and glamour modelling. When I met Cherrise, she was flirting with all of them. She had hoped such work would be a stepping stone to fame, which is far from a new ambition. What is new is that you no longer need to migrate to a major city like New York, London or LA to join the party.

Suzie McFadden has always felt that her home town has held her back. Paisley may be the biggest town in Scotland, but it is still too small for 30-year-old Suzie's ambition. 'I've always felt from a young age that I'm capable of doing big things and I felt like my town …' She pauses. Paisley is still her home after all, and after a whirlwind decade in pursuit of celebrity, it is where she still lives with her parents, even though she's desperate to be back in London. 'I do believe if you want to work in the industry and you wanna like, be in the thick of it, you have to be in London,' she sighs.

Suzie's life has been a long pursuit of offline celebrity. The vivacious and charismatic Scotswoman tried to find fame in the capital three times, and failed each time due to the expense. 'See my first job in London was £14,000 a year,' she tells me. 'I was easily spending maybe £30 a day on food. Not going out or anything.' A friend snuck her onto an interview list at the right-wing *Daily Express* newspaper. The job allowed Suzie to stay in London for a few more months, but she wanted to be the kind of personality tabloids like the *Express* wrote about, not the editorial dogs-body running errands there.

For over a decade, Suzie had bounced between Scotland and London, picking up various bits of media work – reading traffic reports and doing shift work on local radio stations – but that was not where she aspired to be. 'I was not in a good place. It was draining me,' she laments. 'Mentally I was just sad. I felt I was trying so hard. I was getting rejections all the time. I was going in for meetings at different radio stations and saying "yeah, I've done this" and blah blah blah, and it's just like "we don't care". I demoed for Capital Scotland, the breakfast show, and I never got it. Then I demoed for Heart Scotland, I never got that, and then I was just like what am I doing wrong?'

Suzie moved back home to Scotland for good after being diagnosed with depression as a result of her unrealised dreams. 'I went to the doctor's a while back and I had anxiety. I get panic attacks sometimes.' She was approaching 30, living at home with her parents and further away from fame than at any point in her life. While there, she picked up her phone and scrolled through Instagram, where ordinary men and women had built huge platforms for themselves. 'I did start to see the potential in new media, because old media wasn't working out the way I wanted it to.' Old media felt closed and exclusive, but social media appeared to be a meritocracy that rewarded personality and patience – and if you didn't have either of those, then sex appeal was more powerful than both.

'When I was 18, I did a topless photo shoot,' she tells me. 'I wanted to be in *The Sun* and I wanted to be on page 3 because everyone was like "you've got really great boobs, you should do this" … My whole, whole life, I've been, since I was in high school, I was busty. In my year book it said most likely to be a glamour model? Suzanne McFadden. Someone wrote that about me before I left school because I was like this voluptuous busty girl, so I've always been it. I tried to hide it for parts of my life, I tried to hide it but I learnt that I can't.'

Suzie's Instagram page had always been generic and anonymous. There were pictures of her at festivals, drinking tea, and occasionally out on the town as an ordinary twenty-something. On her 29th birthday, she posted two shiny fluorescent pink balloons with the hashtag #HBDMe. She had already launched a YouTube channel, where she posted vlogs about her dating life that she hoped to monetise, but most posts got no more than a few hundred views. She wanted more attention. So she transformed her online presence.

She began taking semi-nude pictures of herself and posting them on Instagram with promotional hashtags regularly used by pornographic accounts: #BBW #CurvyGirl #Hourglass #PlusSize. In the photographs, she leans over and directs her camera down her cleavage. Men would leave lewd comments, but for the most part Suzie would reply, because the algorithm would then boost the post, meaning more people on Instagram would see it. 'I feel like it creates a snowball effect,' she says. She found herself gaining up to 2,000 followers a day through a series of regimented posts. She tried to add variety, but there was always one main theme. 'You can predict there's going to be a lot of boobs on my page,' she laughs. The more followers she gained, the more she posted. 'I see people around me with 1.2m, 1.5m, 2m followers. I see people that I know on that, so for me … it feels almost like a competition, it does. It gets competitive in your head.'

In under a year, she went from 3,000 followers to 250,000. Another year after that, she had passed half a million. According to Instagram, 95 per cent of her followers were male, and although their surprising top location was Baghdad, Iraq, that did not appear to bother Suzie. 'I believe it's so hard to get people's attention these days because we're losing our capacity. There's so many things going on so if you get attention, take it. Attention is money.' Self-objectification is built into our social media use, and for women like Suzie, it has become a principal source of income. She regularly tagged fast-fashion brands until they started giving her free clothes. Eventually, Fashion Nova's plus-size range began gifting her skimpy outfits and even paid her to post. She was now a NovaBabe, and that was just the start. 'A lot of lingerie brands contact me now and I get all of this because obviously I'm a busty girl. I'm going to Ibiza in a couple of weeks and I've got them all saying "can we give you clothes for when you're on the beach?" because they know they are going to get a lot of attention!'

When Suzie relocated to London in her early twenties, she had inherited a significant amount of money that she frittered away trying to cover her costs. 'My dad's like "you're so stupid, you should have put that down on a house,"' she says. Now, in her thirties, she agreed with him, and so was aggressively growing her Instagram account in the hope of making the money back – and more. In the meantime, her wardrobe was fast running out of space. Her father became increasingly bemused by his daughter's new popularity with the postman. 'My dad doesn't get what I do at all. He loves me but he doesn't understand this whole world. He's like "why do you have another package, are you gonna get done for fraud!" That's what he says to me all the time.'

The most reliable chunk of Suzie's money comes not from the companies besieging her with packages but from the besotted men who stalk her online. A male following is less lucrative to brands who sell to women, and so Suzie has not managed to secure the same lucrative deals as female influencers with more female fans. This is how Instagram became her stepping stone to OnlyFans. Instagram is the shop door and OnlyFans is the checkout.

Suzie has utilised both OnlyFans and Patreon. In the early days, she says, she had not even thought much about selling images of herself until she realised she could monetise the initial unwanted attention. 'I started getting messages like "oh my God, I can see your nipples in that top" and I was like hmm, that's not the way I wanted it to be but then when I was making money out of it, I was thinking right, okay. Loads of people asked me, "Do you have OnlyFans?" I got asked that all the time.'

The site's use by hardcore porn stars discouraged her at first, and she initially opted for a Patreon account instead, which allowed her most fanatical followers to pay for even racier photographs and personalised messages. She later launched a page on OnlyFans too, as more mainstream figures migrated to the platform, although she made it clear that she drew the line at nudes and explicit adult content, describing her pictures as 'not what I would put on Instagram. I don't do topless, it might just be something that's showing my body off a bit better.' At her peak, she had 70 patrons willing to pay money monthly to see more of her. She was making thousands from pictures she would otherwise have posted for free. 'At the start of this year I was like I wanna make as much money as possible. I'm 30 years old now. I wanna buy a house eventually. I don't wanna be broke my whole life … I wanna pay my mum and dad back.'

Her busiest day is Valentine's Day. The subscription to her Patreon account surges. Men spending the day alone pay her for loving messages. 'I've got one guy who is like, clinically depressed and I just know if I like, speak to him and stuff it picks him up,' she says. She is providing emotional labour as well as soft pornography.

Moderate sex work of this nature has become so safe and effortless online that Suzie has become one of many young women to stumble into it by accident, selling photos of themselves and feigning intimacy with lonely men and women. The paradox of the internet age is that never have individuals been so well connected yet felt so alone. This has boosted demand for the services Suzie provided. If you are an alienated man, you can pay a woman to take an interest in you, and as an extra she will throw in some semi-nude pictures to help you pass the time. In the past, Suzie worked for the *Express* newspaper, then owned by Richard Desmond, who had made billions off the bodies of young women through the porn magazines he once published. Now, millennial women and teenagers can cut out the ageing middleman (although the owners of OnlyFans may beg to differ).

Suzie estimates that in a good month she can make up to £4,000, but although she is thrilled about the money, this is not what she set out to do with her life. She drew inspiration from Kim Kardashian and from former British page 3 girl Katie Price, who became popular after a stint on the reality TV show *I'm a Celebrity ... Get Me Out of Here*. 'People fell in love with her. She changed her whole image. What I'm saying is, you can always change. You gotta have something about you in the first place' is how Suzie sees it. Both Kim and Katie reinvented themselves as model mothers and household personalities popular with women. Suzie was adamant that she could do the same.

Models have built huge followings under the banner of body positivity, but the term also gives a sense of moral purpose to entrepreneurs like Suzie whose bodies have become part of their trade. Suzie, in her own words, is 'not a skinny girl'. She knows what it is to be body-shamed online, and like many models trying to build a following, she added 'body positive activist' to her Instagram biography in order to tap into the burgeoning women's movement sweeping across Instagram. Where Suzie differs is that she can admit that her primary motivation is money and attention, although she does like the idea of being revered for something other than partial nudity.

'I had it in my thing but I took it off because ... I want all people to accept who they are but I don't feel that's the right title for me.' I ask her why she added it in the first place. 'All plus-size girls have it as their thing!' she replies.

'I want people to be inspired by me but I know you don't think I'm inspirational!' I'm surprised by the comment. Why does it matter if she's seen as inspirational? But then again, it isn't much different to how we all curate our online identities to seem more intelligent or interesting.

After removing 'body positive activist' from her biography, Suzie updated her page. She now defines herself as a 'digital entrepreneur', a desirable moniker in a world where leading businessmen like Elon Musk and Richard Branson are exalted like sportsmen. Politicians and popular culture have attached heroism to entrepreneurship, and Suzie desires the same acclaim as a businesswoman enabled by social media. After all, digital sex work is increasingly an influencer enterprise.

Women's work

The internet has changed the possibilities of women's work. According to Jennifer Quigley-Jones, who runs Digital Voices, one of London's leading influencer agencies, 'there are more female influencers [than men] and they tend to get paid better [than men] because their work is often more commercial. Purely commercial, like fashion or beauty.' But these commercial industries and the influencer scene they depend on are also helping to create a boom in sex work online for young women like Cherrise, who see it as a stepping stone.

Although Suzie sold sexually provocative pictures, she did not appear to see it as sex work, or indeed anything other than a temporary way to turn an income online before her other careers took off. For her it was digital entrepreneurialism, and she was empowered. Yet for all the autonomy technology has allowed young women, it is notable that the main platforms they use, such as OnlyFans, Patreon and even Instagram, were founded by men and enable exploitative behaviour.

A former sex worker turned anonymous blogger calling herself 'Rae C Story' described this new climate as 'a homing ground for masculine gratification, distorted to look like female empowerment though exposure, manufacture and branding'.[3] Rogue companies owned by men mine pictures posted to Instagram by women with hashtags such as #Curvy and illegally reuse them on pornographic websites on an industrial scale. Suzie found herself a victim of this theft and posted an emotional video about her fight to remove pictures stolen from her Instagram without her consent. The internet has been credited with making sex work safer by giving women more autonomy. However, more often than not, the platforms that influencers use are not a safe space at all.

During the pandemic, digital sex work became a legitimate stop along the way to a brand deal. Yet this new frontier still has to reckon with just how empowering it claims to be. Are those launching themselves on these new platforms pioneering entrepreneurs or are they workers in need of greater protection and rights from technology companies making the real money? Sex work on OnlyFans and Instagram has made some young women wealthy and given them flexibility. However, the stories of riches are the exception rather than the rule and the financial rewards are only a part of the story.

While Suzie and Cherrise considered it easy money, according to Rae C, the emotional labour of feigning a desirable persona can be backbreaking. 'We performed our happiness: empowered, sexy and comfortable in our roles as sponges for immediate male satisfaction, whilst pushing our maladies and distresses down the sides of the sofa. Women I knew over the years developed new psychological or emotional complaints and addictions, or predispositions that had already been seeded began to fully develop.' This haunting prose makes me wonder what the real toll of influencer culture is when every day young men and women find even more elaborate ways to be bought and sold online. The cost of this fast-growing way of life is yet to be really tallied. Sex work is just one way that influencer culture can be understood as the consumption of people. In all influencer work there is no real retreat into anonymity, something that is afforded to most other workers, and the only way to clock off is to log off, an impossible task as social media is both our place of work and where our social life is. The emotional labour of influencer work – the management of feelings and expressions for professional gain – never ends.

4

SMILE (OR FIGHT), YOU'RE ON CAMERA

If you really want to witness just how the rewards of the social media attention economy are warping human behaviour, then take a trip to California. The pursuit of fame, fortune and followers has long been part of the state's DNA, but social media has accelerated the Cali way of life into an extreme sport, especially in its booming community of IRL ('in real life') streamers. Unlike Instagrammers, who carefully filter and curate an unobtainable aesthetic, IRL streamers film themselves all day every day without filter and invite you to be a permanent spectator. Sometimes they even give you the control pad. This sounds simple enough, but the lengths they go to to garner attention and money sometimes border on the illegal and surpass the unethical. Increasingly, the questions that social media now tempts its users with are: What would you be willing to do for attention if it paid? How far would you go for a cheque?

In the summer before the COVID pandemic hit, I travelled to Los Angeles to see the impact of this incentive of the attention economy on the most desperate. I was meeting Ebenezer Lembe, a West African migrant who had gone from being homeless to earning a living being racially abused on the internet. Ebenezer, or Ebz (pronounced E-B-Z), is a dark-skinned man of medium height and slight muscular build, with a shaved head. His place in America is a stroke of luck – or destiny, depending on how you look at it. He was born in Cameroon in the early 1980s and was raised between the cities of Yaoundé and Douala. The latter is a place with hard roads and large homes for those with money, a place where 'everyone is going to school. Everyone is trying to be something,' according to Ebz. For most middle-class Cameroonians, that means the employment holy trinity of lawyer, doctor or engineer, but Ebz had no interest in any of those respectable jobs: he wanted to be a star.

Ebz is the son of Matilda, a hard-working nurse, and an absent father, and has always dreamed of making music and entertaining. His influences are American rap, R&B and Hollywood, worlds in which the spoils are split among the fortunate – but then Ebz has always felt lucky. His ticket to America was the result of winning a lottery he did not even know he was playing. His mother had a sister living in Nigeria who completed visa applications for the entire family via the lottery system in the 1990s. Today, the chances of being successful in the visa lottery are estimated to be between 1 in 25 and 1 in 75.[1] Against the odds, they won, and Ebenezer was on his way to America.

Now 37 years old, Ebz sounds like he has never lived anywhere else. His voice projects like a newscaster or a Hollywood actor, despite the fact that he arrived in America when he was 18. The US can be harsh towards migrants who bring their home with them in any form, especially through their tongue. Ebz's accent and well-spoken manner is part of why he has always found it so easy to pick up work. His big problem has been keeping it. When he first arrived, he lived in his cousin's cramped house in Alabama. He enrolled in community college to study music management and sound recording, but experienced the isolation common to new migrants. He would drive to college, go to class, go home, repeat. He did manage to make friends, but not the kind his mother approved of. Ebenezer had gone to private school in Cameroon, paid for by his affluent uncle, but now, in Alabama, he befriended small-time drug dealers and spent his days involved in the minutiae of street life. From petty disputes to low-level dealing himself, he was, in his own words, 'making no money being a truant'. He admits he would have been better off working at Starbucks.

At least that way he would have avoided a series of run-ins with the law.

Twice he was pursued by police officers. The first time he managed to escape, but the second time he was placed under arrest, a risky event for a migrant. A drug offence could result in deportation, but according to Ebz, the amount was so small he was able to plead guilty to intent to use rather than supply. He was placed on probation for five years and made to do an anti-drugs programme. It could have been far worse. He had gotten lucky again.

Ebz returned to college, but eventually dropped out. He managed to pick up bits of shift work, and when he came home, he would write songs, record them, burn them onto CDs and then give them away at the nearby gas station, hoping to build a fan base. 'All I'm doing is writing songs, watching TV and doing what I can to just maintain. Life is hard. I'm broke as fuck,' he recalls.

In his late twenties, after years of failure, Ebz rolled the dice and followed the well-trodden road to Los Angeles, but was faced with the challenge of having nowhere to live and dwindling money. He found a halfway house for recovering alcoholics and drug dependents in Long Beach, but he had to fake an addiction to qualify. He had perfected his act from observing addicts in Alabama. The rent was $450, which meant that after making his first payment he only had $150 of his savings left. The next day he found his first job in Los Angeles, as a food server on Ocean Boulevard.

When I've met and spoken to Ebz, he has only been extraordinarily polite, with far better manners than mine, but beneath his charm, he admits he has a temper that has sometimes been his downfall. A dispute with a fellow resident in the halfway house led to an 'altercation', and Ebz was asked to leave. He had no car and still hadn't even received his first pay cheque. He managed to find a homeless shelter, the Weingart Center, but that was all the way downtown, at best an hour's drive away, on Skid Row, the infamous home of America's down-and-outs. Outside the hostel are rows of tents that extend for blocks. The residents are made up largely of the disabled black poor: a picture of dystopia against the moneyed utopia California presents to the world. Ebenezer was now among America's most destitute.

His change of address soon became a change of job, too. He had gotten the server gig with a promise that he would bring in the documents that proved he was eligible to work in the US, but he had lost them somewhere between Alabama and Los Angeles. When he was unable to provide them after several weeks, he was asked to leave.

A chance encounter at the shelter led him to pick up work collecting signatures on a petition for state-wide policies to lower college tuition fees. A gentleman who was doing the same job introduced him to the coordinator, an elderly woman. The pay offered was 25 cents per signature. The job required him to accost strangers who had no interest in talking to him. 'I was going up to people to have a full-blown conversation in which I needed their signature to make 25 cents,' he laughs.

One day, Ebz made his usual phone call to the office to tell the coordinator that he was about to make the three-hour journey to collect his meagre pay cheque, in case she was going out, but the woman who answered was not the elderly woman who had employed him. Unbeknown to him, his de facto employer had died, and he was told there was no money to collect. 'You ever been in pain and you scream so much that you're like fuck it? That's how I felt that day. I can't feed myself. I've lost my documents.' What am I going to do now? he thought.

Ebz borrowed some money from a friend and found a job at the burger chain Wendy's. He even got a second job as a server elsewhere too. He managed to save enough to buy a used Honda, but he was past 30, wondering where his youth had gone and pondering what success looked like for a man of his age. He was not married; he was not even making music. He was bouncing from dead-end job to dead-end job. He estimates he has had over 15 jobs since moving to LA, but it is likely to be many more, because he cannot remember how many he has had in the past 18 months, let alone the past 10 years. At his most desperate, he even turned to selling knock-off jeans. Ebz had found a spot next to a gas station in the Valley. When he arrived to set up at 6 a.m., he caught sight of his reflection. He had migrated to America for a better life, and here he was selling T-shirts on the road like a market boy back home in Cameroon.

After a decade in LA, Ebenezer was sliding towards 40 and operating in the gig economy on the range of new apps that removed worker guarantees in exchange for flexible hours and on-demand work. He joined the hot new ride-sharing app Uber as a driver. To do the job efficiently, he downgraded his beloved champagne Mercedes for a uniform black Toyota Prius. He hated Uber but loved the time it afforded him to make music again. He was still hoping he might be shown attention by somebody who mattered. He had never been granted his 15 minutes of fame, but at least he was in better spirits now that he was recording in his spare time, and he even took some of his new music for company in between rides. He was in a surprisingly good place when his smartphone blinked one day and he accepted the next job. 'Pick up Paul,' the message from Uber read.

What happened next could only have been dreamt up in the Hollywood Hills. Ebz was about to pick up an infamous influencer and livestreamer, a man who was at the helm of the so-called Purple Army, otherwise known as the CX Network, home to some of the most toxic people on the internet.

Build a cult

Subtlety has no place in a world where extreme behaviour reaps the greatest rewards. Nowhere is this more apparent than in livestreaming, which takes the drama of tried-and-tested reality TV to depraved and voyeuristic new levels due to the immediacy the medium provides. One of livestreaming's most notorious players is twenty-something American Paul Denino, better known by his alias Ice Poseidon. Denino, who sits at the intersection of the prankster bro culture captured in TV shows like *Jackass* and the toxic corner of online gaming, is the king of his personal fiefdom, the CX Network, a digital channel whose fanatical followers can log on to follow his wild antics in real life (IRL) alongside a revolving door of characters he turns into entertainment for his audience. Fans of the channel are attracted by its calling card of misogynistic, racist and extreme acts – all meticulously stoked by Denino in the name of 'content'. IRL streaming communities rely on an influencer business model that incentivises behaviour so dangerous it has even put lives in danger.

Like most livestreamers, Denino's life online started in gaming. Under the moniker Ice Poseidon, created by a random name generator, he became addicted to the fantasy game RuneScape, according to a profile in the *New Yorker*. In high school, he was a social recluse, but online he made friends with other gamers and enjoyed playing pranks on them. He uploaded his videos to YouTube, but his life changed after he set up an account with the livestreaming platform Twitch. The site, which allows viewers to make financial donations to the streamers who entertain them the most, has been hailed as the birthplace of professional livestreaming. Here Denino found not just followers but a family, albeit a dysfunctional one, and he gave his fast-growing fan base decision-making power over his life as they watched online, allowing them to choose the music he played, letting them call him, and even calling them back – as long as they paid for the pleasure.

When he was made redundant as a cook after leaving high school, he packed his bags and moved to East Hollywood.[2] He filled his apartment with video equipment and it was open to anyone who wanted to drop by – an arrangement that started his 'collection' of homeless people, vagabonds and lonely young men. There was a commercial value to his open-door policy: each person who came in joined the livestream, providing an unscripted storyline for his viewers. The constant stream of oddball characters generated news and gossip that kept his audience multiplying into the tens of thousands. A news thread he created on the website Reddit had hundreds of thousands of subscribers trading memes, insults and suggestions. The thread regularly violated the site's terms with racist and sexist language. Posts openly expressed hatred of women, and use of the 'N' word was frequent among the core young white male demographic. Denino himself publicly supported Donald Trump, and many saw the community as a kickback against a liberal agenda and political correctness. He even gave his mob of followers a name: the Purple Army.

The community was aggressively masculine and entitled, and its members had an unhealthy relationship with Denino, who egged them on. He once even published a young woman's number and the Purple Army did what they did best: tormented her with prank calls and abusive messages. But it was not only the viewers who were badly behaved. Denino would film himself trolling the homeless, or humiliating young women in his apartment, cheered on by his male audience, who tipped him more money the cruder he became with his content.

The omniscient Purple Army also found extreme ways to toy with their hero. When Denino livestreamed himself going to a McDonald's, members called the LA Police Department and told them they'd seen a man with a suspect package in a fast-food restaurant, prompting an armed response team to be deployed, a high-stakes prank known in the livestream world as 'swatting'. On another occasion, Denino was on board a flight to Phoenix waiting for the aircraft to take off when the cabin doors burst open and armed law enforcement flooded on board. The airline had received a call that a passenger was carrying an explosive device, and Denino matched the description. It was one of many false claims the Purple Army made so they could watch the fireworks in real time. The Twitch message board would ring like crazy when a swat operation was taking place on Denino's livestream. Tens of messages would be posted per second and donations would pour into his bank account – a sign that the army was entertained and Denino could sleep well. Swatting in a country where police are armed can be distressing and high-risk, but the drama helped Denino to make up to $2,000 a day in tips.

The rise in livestreaming did not just benefit its leading personalities. In 2014, Amazon paid $970m for Twitch, making its developers and early investors rich and richer, respectively.[3] Twitch is now estimated to be worth at least 20 times that. Livestreaming at one point was the hottest cultural trend in video. Instagram introduced a livestream option. So did Facebook. When YouTube created a payment system for viewers to tip livestreamers like you could on Twitch, many professional streamers switched platforms.

Even Denino returned to posting on YouTube with vigour. In 2020, his channel hit 750,000 subscriptions.

It was this strange world that Ebenezer became embroiled in. The aspiring rapper picked Denino up outside his apartment, completely unaware that he was about to feature on Denino's Ice Poseidon livestream, which was being broadcast to thousands of people via his smartphone. 'Is this shoot day? Am I getting shot?' he asked playfully. Denino, ever the showman for his hungry audience, replied, 'Yeah, man. Are you ready?'

As Ebz drove, Denino asked him where he came from. He'd never heard of Cameroon, but when Ebz told him it was in Africa, the livestream message board began to flood with hundreds of derogatory comments from the predominantly white community: 'mah nigga', 'savage', 'KFC', 'watermelon', 'Kony 2010', 'black nikker', 'he has AIDS' were just a few that came within seconds of each other. Ice commented on the bass in Ebz's voice and said he'd make a good Batman, before performing a mock impersonation for the camera: 'I'm the Batman, I'm here from West Africa, I am going to go get my AK-47s that I illegally obtained from Italy.' Ebz looked awkward but played along. The Purple Army loved casual racism. 'The darker knight', said one comment in response to Ice's Batman parody.

The cab ride continued with Ebz apparently in good spirits and Ice in full troll mode. 'I'm glad you're following your dreams, man,' he said, sounding insincere. 'I'm trying to, man. I do music.' Ice asked him what music he made, and Ebz loaded the track then pressed play, rapping along to his own voice with Ice full-blown dancing in the back seat. Unlike the music, Ice had no rhythm, but he appeared to be having fun, and so were the viewers. The stream raced with comments. The most common was the fire emoji: *FIYYAA … actually good … damn, the beat is sick … Str8 fire, new pac … AMAZING … wtf so good.* The Purple Army had selected their latest star.

Ebz was quickly initiated into the CX Network as one of the many waifs and strays Denino picked up. He set up an account and received financial rewards in the form of tips from the Purple Army if he entertained them. To maintain their attention, he even wrote a song called 'The Purple Army', which currently has over 500,000 streams across YouTube and Spotify. 'I wrote the song. I recorded it. I released it. He didn't give a fuck about it but the fans took it and ran with it. The fans ate it up,' Ebz says. He became a regular fixture, making between $75 and $140 a day from viewer donations. He was also invited to the gatherings at Denino's house and group trips where conflict between guests was stoked to create content for viewers. 'If I'm making money it's because I'm arguing with somebody,' he says. 'You know the money is based on the emotions of the day, right? If nothing is happening you're not making any money … You never made money when you were peaceful.'

Unlike many of the other CX characters, Ebz was not raised on the internet. He often cut a bizarre figure as a black man in his mid thirties among a group of young white internet kids in their twenties and teens who regularly used the N-word and compared him to a gorilla. When he turned the song he had written for the Purple Army into a music video, members of the network hoisted bananas and fried chicken alongside him. Viewers accused him of leeching off Denino to buy watermelons.

Ebz appeared to play along, even calling Denino 'my nigga', but on occasion he reacted. He challenged another streamer dubbed 'Jim Carrey' for saying the N-word. 'I can say whatever I want,' replied Jim. Ebz responded with two right hooks to the body and Jim shut up. That was not the only fight he was involved in either. He had a series of arguments with several other characters, including British YouTuber Sam Pepper, a former *Big Brother* contestant accused of sexually harassing women on camera during so-called pranks.[4] The pair detested each other and even came to blows.

Although viewers were entertained by Ebz, they relentlessly targeted him on the message board, and regularly sent racially abusive messages on his own stream. However, like his tolerance for the characters he collaborated with but could not stand, he saw being insulted as part of his lucrative new career. 'Right now if you look at my computer screen or my YouTube channel it will cost you $3–5 to do something,' he explains. 'If you wanna say wassup, if you wanna play me a record, or if you wanna say it out loud, the computer can say it for you or you can pay $5 to say it yourself. You can come online and say "hey fuckface, I hate your mutha fucking ass" and you can pay $5 to do that. Or pay $3 and the computer will do it for you.'

He understands that he is effectively paid to be insulted. 'I know it's crazy. It's like a fucking …' He trails off as he thinks back to his battles with homelessness, low pay and not knowing where his next meal was coming from. 'YouTube is child's play. Your landlord kicking you out because you can't pay rent, that's a problem!' He was close to rock bottom many times in California. Making a good living thanks to white teenagers paying him to call him a nigger? No problem. 'I'd still rather do this than work a 9–5 somewhere … that's why I feel blessed,' he says. 'When I worked at Mercedes people were like "nice job". I dressed well but I was extremely broke. Now people are like you look like a loser but I'm travelling whenever I want. It all comes down to checks and balances. What's in your account?'

Several years after Denino started streaming, the toxicity of the Purple Army led to his suspension from Twitch, and his community news thread was removed from Reddit. According to Ebz, Denino could still be earning $50,000 a month, mostly in donations, but he has turned to other ways to make money. His jewel was the CX Network, where he exhibited the characters he'd collected. Each hoped that exposure there would increase their own daily tips. For Ebz, the difference was marginal. 'If I wasn't on the network I'd get 50 viewers and on the network I'd get 70, 80 maybe 100 viewers. So I'd make like $75 and when I'm on the network I'd see an extra 40 bucks, something like that.' Even on the network he was not earning enough to quit his day job. Denino generated income from being able to claim ownership of the CX Network itself. In contrast, others on the website were struggling to make ends meet. 'It gives him more credibility, gives him more respect ... If I was him, I'd do the same thing,' says Ebz.

The CX Network website, like all platforms, is reliant on users and viewers to generate attention. The website's software then extracts data from those who are watching, with the aim of personalising digital adverts targeting them. The model, invented by Google, was one the CX Network never managed to fully imitate even when Denino began to take it more seriously. He presented the community like an entrepreneurial start-up and himself as a businessman, but at heart it was still just a mob of trolls built around a demagogue. Denino would troll the people he needed to be stars and would regularly take them off the stream at a whim, which could significantly affect what little money they were making. 'You know it was definitely a display of power,' says Ebz. Removing a streamer would generate gossip in the community, like a soap opera killing off a lead character before bringing them back from the dead for dramatic effect.

The Purple Army's entertainment was Denino's financial gain, even if it came at Ebenezer's expense. 'He definitely used me. I was never even a person to him. I was an idea that could be tolerated, entertained and turned into money,' Ebz says coolly. He feels both exploited and beholden to the man who gave him a new career on the bottom rung of the digital economy.

Work on the internet can be even more exploitative than work offline. Social media platforms are reliant on users for their attention and data. Every time you log into Facebook or Instagram, the platform studies how long you are online for and what keeps you plugged in. On YouTube, a creator or influencer able to consistently generate attention is paid a cut in the form of ad revenue, and when these individuals build followings and graduate to influencer status, their followers hope to be able to do the same through collaborations with those with more clout, an incentive model with the same rules as a pyramid scheme. If viewer donations have broken the reliance of streamers on the ad revenue from sites like YouTube, they have also created a new dilemma. Streamers are obliged to live a life of performance disguised as authenticity. Increasingly, creators are rewarded for misleading their viewers.

The CX Network was not the only business Denino incorporated. He launched another venture he called 'Scuffed'. In Silicon Valley, entrepreneurs hope to strike it rich by convincing a few wealthy people to back them, but in LA, Denino was turning to his followers to raise $2m. He told them that 'in order for investors to make their money back, what we do is we grow the company to a certain point and then we have other investors come in and obviously they invest their money as well. Hopefully when we get more than $2m invested, the other investors get their $2m back and then we have more money for the company or shit like that.'[5] His description is of a company that pays investors from the money gained from new investors, once again like a pyramid scheme. What he was describing was also fraudulent, a charge he denied. But for Denino, every relationship was an attempted transaction.

In summer 2019, the LA sun was uncharacteristically late, but it was out in full force the July day Ebz and I decided to hike up Hollywood's Runyon Canyon. Ebz had brought his livestream and his selfie stick. 'How long will you be streaming for?' I asked. 'All day,' he laughed. He invited me to feature on camera, but I declined. His viewers could already hear my voice, and even that sparked them into a frenzy, demanding Ebz reveal his 'boyfriend' and sending a barrage of homophobic messages. As we walked up the dusty trail under the midday sun, I was sweating, and not just from the heat. Ebz had been the victim of swatting several times, and we were two dark-skinned black men in a city whose police department had shot and killed 14 people already that year. A flippant false call from his fans could put us at risk. I was nervous, but Ebz was relaxed. He was so focused on talking to his viewers that he didn't see the dog turd approaching. 'Watch out for the shit,' I warned. He didn't hear me in time and stepped into it.

During our hour-long hike, Ebz had the camera streaming the entire time but made just $14, only a few cents more than California's minimum wage. Despite this, he is content with the path he's on. The entire CX Network was shut down following a police raid. 'It was always bad vibes,' he told me. 'I never felt comfortable. Let me rephrase that. When I was on the network I was doing Uber, right? I'm off the network, I don't do Uber any more. The more I delved into myself, the more I started enjoying my own livestream. Then I started making more money. Now I make more money than on the network.' By then, he had been streaming for 380 days. It had taken him around 270 to no longer need the income from Uber to pay his bills.

To me, his job entertaining an audience of vitriolic young white men appeared like the digital equivalent of a modern-day minstrel show, where he shucked and jived for a dollar. 'Every job is shucking and jiving,' he protested. 'If you're a telemarketer you're shucking and jiving. If you're a car salesman you're shucking and jiving.' These were all jobs he had done for low pay. 'You know what I consider shucking and jiving? In my eyes, it's doing what I'm asked to do. If I'm asked to sit here and answer every single phone call, that's shucking and jiving because I don't wanna do it … so now I'm in a world where someone gives me $3 just to say "wassup". I know it's crazy [but] that's why I'm just very grateful. The world does not even realise this. Most people are still in the mentality "I've got to work Monday to Sunday 9–5 to fucking pay the bills." You just have to be smart.'

I asked him if he had ever sent money back over racial abuse. 'If I want to. I usually don't. I say fuck you and I keep it.' We laugh. 'Keep in mind I've worked so many 9–5 jobs I know what my plight in life is. I know what I've put all my efforts in and I've finally found that thing that gave me an opportunity to have people listen to what I make.' He can now make up to $1,000 a day in donations from as few as 50 viewers, sometimes from just one entertained donor, although the amount varies. 'I have many $1,000 days. I have many $150 days.' In addition to donations, the rap songs he has made about the Purple Army have generated him a monthly revenue peaking at $400 from his 21,132 listeners on Spotify, and over 1.2 million total plays. He no longer feels the precarity he did when he lived on Skid Row, nor does he believe that dignity can be found in work. In his mind he has something better. He finally has attention, or 'clout'.

However, while Ebz is content with his lot and aware of the Faustian bargain he has made, other members of the CX Network were easily exploited by Denino, who used their own ambitions against them.

'I'm nothing without my following'

Jessy Taylor was barely old enough to legally drink when Denino and Sam Pepper recruited the 20-year-old to join the network. Jessy had held an obsessive desire to be inter-net-famous ever since she was in high school. She had met Pepper offline trying to gatecrash a party attended by A-list YouTubers at the infamous 'Clout House', Hollywood's most famous influencer home. Instead of getting inside, she had ended up among Denino's collection of weirdos and misfits.

Jessy sold herself as an ex-stripper turned escort, and Denino thrived on using her for sexual content for his legion of incel (involuntarily celibate) followers. On one occasion, he coerced her into kissing a far older homeless man, but worse was to come. He had added a robot to his stream that he allowed viewers to control for a fee. He attached a black dildo to the robot and told Jessy to have sex with it in front of his viewers.

Wearing a black bra and blue knickers, Jessy giggled nervously as she sat on her heels and put the dildo to her lips. 'I'm the craziest bitch in the world to be doing this,' she said. 'Go buy my premium [sexy videos],' she added. She then received a cue and removed her bra. 'You want me to fuck it right now?' she asked Denino. She pulled her knickers to the side and then inserted the robotic dildo. 'I'm not used to black dick,' she said, smirking.

On Twitch, not only can viewers make donations, but they can pay to send computerised voice notes. You type the message and the software translates it into a mechanical voice. As members of the Purple Army paid to have sex with Jessy via a robot, their abusive messages were read out on the livestream for all to hear: 'Listen here, you drug-addicted scumbag whore, stop fucking a robot for clout, you nasty bitch.' Another member sent: 'She's going to claim the robot got her pregnant and move into Ice's place.'

Jessy's public mockery by Pepper and Denino for the Purple Army has made her a regular recipient of abuse. 'I get called a slut maybe like 600 times a day just for existing,' she tells me. But despite this, she credits Pepper as 'the one who discovered me'. 'He's changed my life. Without Sam

Pepper I wouldn't be here now. I don't know what I would be doing.'

After the dildo video, Jessy's Instagram exploded and her following grew to over 100,000, which allowed her to make an income selling promotional shout-outs and links to the pages where she sold nudes. 'People buying my stuff, that's literally how I make my money. They can buy swipe-ups [a link from her Instagram page to your business]. I get a lot of fans who send me gift cards and a lot of fans who wanna spoil me.'

The CX Network may have given her a platform to grow her social media following, but the Purple Army also could exert pressure to take it away. Jessy's sexual bravado titillated and entertained the network's young white male viewers, but it also angered them. The Purple Army were a fraternity online, composed of male gamers, but offline they were isolated. They were men who desired women who had no interest in them. Jessy was everything they hated: a young woman who appeared to be profiting from her own sexuality at their expense. In retaliation, they mounted a campaign to mass-report her page to Instagram for violations.

The platform deleted her account, leading Jessy into a public breakdown. But in the influencer economy, drama is always to be monetised, and so on 5 April 2019, a tearful Jessy took out her camera, fixed her ponytail and began to record a monologue for YouTube with the caption 'STOP REPORTING MY INSTAGRAM ACCOUNT':

'I'm in LA, I'm in LA because I want to be on Instagram … I'm nothing without my following. I'm *nothing* without my following and when people try to hate on me, report me, I'm literally trying to be a better fucking person. I want to say to everybody who's been reporting me, think twice because you're ruining my life because I make all of my money online, all of it, and I don't want to lose that and I know people like to see me, be down and be like them and be like the 90 per centers, the people that work 9–5. That is not me. I am in LA to *not* be like that.'

At last count, the original YouTube post had a humble two million views, but the video has been seen by far more people than that. The original was duplicated and syndicated by media around the world, from Britain's biggest tabloids, *The Sun* and the *Daily Mail*, to the *New Zealand Herald* and *Perth Now* in Australia. Jessy's name went viral as the archetypal self-promoting influencer. She was the girl who would do anything to be popular: the girl who 'fucked a robot'. The world laughed when the video went viral and trolled her, but that was okay: she much preferred being hated over being ignored. 'If you don't have haters you ain't poppin',' she told me.

Even more importantly, her new virality produced a welcome payday after she had spent her first months in LA covering mounting bills with sex work. 'I never need to do that shit any more. I was doing that to do what I'm doing now. I never wanted to do prostitution and stripping long-term. I did it as I knew once I become Instagram famous I'm gonna be out of this bitch. I was just waiting on the day I went viral like the other day, that just secured it for life. I was just waiting on my day to say *fuck this*. That's what I was waiting for and I got it.'

Jessy's YouTube page is monetised. This means she is one of the many YouTubers paid per 1,000 views from adverts YouTube run on her videos. The payment per view varies wildly for YouTube creators, but back then it was around $18 per 1,000 views. This means Jessy's two million views could have earned her up to $36,000, the equivalent of raising a deposit for a house from three minutes of tears. 'If I don't get the account back, I'm not even tripping,' she told me. 'I've made more money with just this video than I have in a while.'

After going viral, Jessy paraded her winnings online like a miner who had struck gold. She has started multiple Instagram accounts since, and even after the virality faded, her following bounced back. 'Even though I got my account deleted I still have my loyal fans, my YouTube following, which is just as valued.' Despite this, none of her new videos have had anywhere near the exposure of her online melt-down. For many of her new followers on the platform, she was a figure of ridicule who they trolled, rather than an influencer whose life they cheered from the sidelines. She believed her viral moment would make her '100 times bigger' and that she would have as long a career as iconic internet celebrity, heiress and reality TV star Paris Hilton. However, just months after her video hit two million, Jessy was back posting videos of her stripping and promoting exotic dance clubs, a job she had said she never wanted to do again.

When I asked her about her experience of pornographic sex work, she denied ever doing it. 'I don't plan on ever doing porn in my life and when people ask me that I wanna slap them. I will never do porn. Once you do it, you're fucked.' Despite this, as of writing there is a video of Jessy still posted on Pornhub.

Jessy told herself that she had never done porn. Ebz told himself that all work was 'shucking and jiving' to deal with performing for racists. Online delusion is a necessity when the reality is so unflattering. In a world where we are encouraged to fake it, the first person you have to convince is yourself. Self-deception is the first step in an economy that thrives off the need to present such demeaning work as worthwhile. After that, everyone else is easier to fool.

The real winners

Anaheim in Orange County was put on the map by Disney in 1955 with the creation of the iconic resort Disneyland.

But when I visited in 2019, it wasn't the famous mouse that was the main attraction. Queues of young people snaked outside Disneyland heading not into the theme park but into the convention centre next door. Anaheim Convention Center was hosting VidCon, the world's biggest convention of YouTubers, on its 10th anniversary.

VidCon was founded in 2009 by brothers Hank and John Green. The millennials were early adopters of vlogging on YouTube. On their Vlogbrothers channel, they documented their lives and produced educational explainer videos, amassing millions of followers along the way with their unique brand of curious-nerd content. Ten years on, the Green brothers were YouTuber elder statesmen. I met Hank, the younger brother, who was in charge of the business network making YouTube content.

'When I and a lot of those people [YouTubers] started making YouTube videos there were no advertisements, there was no way to make money … We thought – we would say – that we were doing it because we loved it, but really we were doing it because we were getting attention, growing something that was interesting. And so the value we were getting, we might now call influence because …' he slows, 'we have words for it now, but no one was getting paid.'

The times have changed. When Jessy Taylor generated thousands of dollars from a viral YouTube video in which she cried about her deleted Instagram account, the money she made came from Google AdSense, which administers the payments from monetised YouTube videos. For every \$1 spent for an advert shown on a video like Jessy's, YouTube keeps 45 cents,[6] so if Jessy took home \$36,000, YouTube made just under \$30,000 from her tears. If that's how much the company made from one woman mining the drama in her life for attention over three minutes, then the 576,000 hours of video uploaded every day makes YouTube a gold mine with unlimited reserves.

In 2020, YouTube's ad revenue surpassed \$19.6bn, and its holding company Alphabet posted total ad revenue of \$146.92bn.[7] In the same year, its rival Facebook posted revenue of \$86bn,[8] with a quarter coming from Instagram's huge growth.[9] The only reason YouTube and Instagram make such astonishing money is due to the pull of the influencers and creators we spend our time watching.

VidCon10 was a reflection of this new digital ecosystem, a habitat now flushed with corporate money. Even the convention itself had been bought for an undisclosed fee by the media multinational Viacom, who have collected lucrative media hubs like infinity stones. The deal meant the Green brothers never needed to work again. According to Hank, the event is now almost unrecognisable. The conference had an estimated 75,000 attendees, each paying up to \$850 for a single ticket, with sponsors spending obscene amounts to engage with them. An insider source told me the unicorn technology company Airtable paid $75,000 for a small media area of no more than four square metres in the industry section of the conference. The number of exhibitors was in the hundreds. VidCon and its new owners were raking it in. The pull of the annual conference remains unmatched. Even Ebz turned up to livestream until a team of security guards seized him after a hoax call. He was not the only IRL livestreamer present either. It felt like every video influencer in LA was making plans to head down to meet fans, search for collaborations and make content.

The technology companies took turns to sell themselves on sponsored panels, and children trying to launch careers as YouTubers dragged their tired parents to seminars on how to grow their audience and sell their merchandise. I saw no seminars on exploitation or tackling abusive communities, and the Big Tech companies themselves were tightly guarded. After Instagram presented its new features for influencers, an obnoxious and prissy press officer fobbed off my interview request.

At VidCon 2019, the migration to the app TikTok had already begun. A year later, talented Gen Z video makers had powered the Chinese-owned platform to a valuation of $50bn by creating ingenious videos that kept audiences scrolling on the site.[10] The success of TikTok had created another gold rush, and at VidCon it felt like everything and everyone was for sale. In the past there was a taboo among

YouTubers and early content creators around charging and making money. The internet was a free parking space from America's overbearing consumerism. Today, the community of YouTubers behind the conference, like most places on the internet, has given in. Online communities are now commodities, and online relationships are valued by how easy they are to monetise.

VidCon had become bigger and more impressive than the Green brothers could have envisaged when they founded it, but the conversations were primarily driven by how to generate more money and business. The new corporate pressure on the event had even caused a rift between the brothers. John, the elder of the two, had retreated from YouTube and VidCon in search of the intimacy he used to find online. He still made occasional YouTube videos for their cult channel but now found refuge in his best-selling writing, his family, and offline friendships first made on the internet.

In the industry bar at VidCon, John blended into the background, a feat unthinkable in the early days of the conference, but such was the scale of the extravaganza, even the co-founder could fall into anonymity. Today, the event stands literally shoulder to shoulder with Disneyland as an embodiment of the new social order in the entertainment industry. What united them was that both were selling versions of the old Californian dream: that fantasy can bring you fame and fortune. California makes our films, makes our smartphones, runs our software, designs our hardware, processes our search queries, curates our lives and provides the fantasy that we can all make it. Most of us literally carry a Californian design in our pockets, and it is from this portal that we log into the new world. Whether you live in London, Nairobi, Hong Kong, Paris or Amsterdam, we all live in California now.

5

WORK FROM HOME:
ASK ME HOW

The world has been migrating online for the past 30 years, but no event in history has made living and working online a necessity like the 2020 COVID-19 pandemic. As a result, the titans of tech and ecommerce like Amazon and Google saw their share prices rocket while poverty and unemployment grew rapidly throughout the world. In 2020, the video-conferencing service Zoom increased its share price fourfold. As Amazon's revenue rose 40 per cent in a year, the US economy fell by 32 per cent.[1] While tech companies boomed, workers in every other sector began to look over their shoulders waiting for the inevitable news that profit targets would be missed. Company emails praised the efforts of staff with one hand but sharpened the knives with the other.

For all the money generated in tech, the industry has not created the same volume of good jobs in Western economies that last century's most profitable industries did. Social media has enabled a wave of new ecommerce companies, but commerce itself is thousands of years old. The difference is now you are even more reliant on middlemen such as Google or Facebook to generate sales. Those providing the labour for companies like Uber and the food delivery app Deliveroo have been rebranded as entrepreneurs. This is a trend with a far-reaching cultural impact, as ever more people have been encouraged to think of themselves as sole traders or hustlers, able to make anything happen with the help of a smartphone. In a cruel twist of fate, the new promise of an income from social media has reinvigorated an old, exploitative and discredited model of wealth acquisition, targeting the most precarious. This is network marketing, a pyramid scheme in all but name.

As COVID continued to devastate incomes during 2020, I noticed more posts on social media from estranged friends inviting me to make money from home. However, even before the outbreak hit, an entire generation was already under mounting pressure and in debt. One of the most interesting examples I came across was an auburn-haired woman in her mid twenties who lives on the other side of the world to me.

Rose always knew when her mother was about to undergo a manic episode. First came the increase in spending, then her outlandish claims and the euphoric moods. When her behaviour became too severe to manage, Rose had on more than one occasion taken the difficult decision to have her hospitalised, she told me on an unstable internet phone line.

Rose lives on Australia's west coast, but on Instagram there are no borders. I found her when following a dubious internet company I had become obsessed with that she was promoting. I wanted to know more about how the company worked and sent Rose a message. She instantly messaged back. Rose was open, sociable and exuded fun, but only seven months earlier, this vivacious young woman had become a recluse when she herself was hospitalised after a mental health breakdown. She had refused to answer the phone to friends and barely left her bedroom. 'I was clinically depressed and they put me on antidepressants,' she recounts.

Rose had tried to avoid drugs her entire life and hated being medicated. She lived with the chronic fear that recreational drugs and excessive alcohol might trigger the mental health problems that had surrounded her parents. Bipolar disorder was a challenge for her mother, and her father had been diagnosed with schizophrenia. Now, Rose was worried that the drugs she had been prescribed confirmed an inherited life sentence. She had initially contested the diagnosis of bipolar that led to her being hospitalised, but once in treatment, things appeared to be slowly improving. She liked her psychiatrist and she was active again: dancing, taking pictures and posting them online with colourful filters and optimistic captions about women's empowerment. On the surface she appeared happier, but her episode in hospital had disrupted her plans. At 25 years old, she had wanted to be further ahead in her life, but after leaving hospital she found herself in conflict with her mum and having to return to her home town, Margaret River.

Rose grew up in a Homeswest house, the Western Australian equivalent of social housing or the American projects, albeit in a picturesque town famed for its surfing and vineyards. In her early twenties, she had left to study social work in Perth, but she never completed the course. 'I studied for social work and came home to Margaret River to care for my mum. That was the only reason I didn't become qualified,' she sighs. According to Rose, her mother's bipolar disorder had 'disrupted my adult life since I left school. I lived in Perth for five years and she kept relapsing.'

After being hospitalised herself, it was a struggle to get back on her feet. Rose became estranged from her family, after contesting their attempt to section her, and had nowhere to live. She was not earning enough to afford the rent of a private room and was too proud to ask for help. 'I could have couch-surfed a bit here and there, which I did at times, but, you know, I never want to be a burden on those friends because they were already offering so much emotional support. I didn't wanna be like, hey guys, I'm homeless can you give me a room to live in?' She may have been reluctant to ask, but when a friend offered her a free room in exchange for childcare and help with her businesses, Rose was grateful.

When I spoke to her, Rose was still on antidepressants but she also self-medicated by posting selfies and risqué videos on Instagram. 'It's like its own form of therapy,' she laughs. 'That's how the whole world, well, my generation, communicates now.' She had always been creative. Throughout her childhood and teens she had trained as a belly dancer, and she told me excitedly about her dreams to one day open a dance school for children. On Instagram she posed and played with the filters and occasionally even posted semi-nude pictures. Her life online was a display of her growing body confidence as she built an internet persona in the manner of the new mini-celebrities she followed, who applied similar techniques to their photographs and social accounts. She posted about feminism, tagged brands she paid for and carefully edited her pictures. After months of introversion, she felt she was transforming into another version of herself. 'It gave me my life back. It gave me a platform and a voice, to make myself feel not alone.'

Rose also hoped her new way of life could earn her a living. In the past it was common for those in need of work to move from the country to the city, or to cross an ocean in pursuit of a better life, but now the easiest and most accessible frontier was accessed by a smartphone and an internet connection. The world of work that Rose had known – a punishing mix of caring and cleaning – had been hostile to her health. It did not pay enough for her to cover her basic costs and took a toll on her body. She needed something new.

'For me, health problems got in my way of being in the workplace in a normal way. I have severe back problems and autoimmune diseases and stuff that means I don't cope well with stress … [I was] absolutely killing myself over those jobs so this is so important to me right now because my end goal is that I become completely self-sufficient and making my own living off of not having to work for other people's companies, so I want to just work for myself.' As she followed more young women who looked like her and took pictures like her but unlike her appeared to make an income from life online, she asked herself 'Why not me too? Why can't I be one of those people that makes money from their phone, like what's stopping me? I'm a normal person but everybody's normal,' she reasoned. 'I can be money. I'm empowered by the idea I can be money.'

She threw herself head-first into growing her profile by courting attention with positive posts about her life. 'It just becomes addictive in this culture that you would want more followers or more likes on your pics or comments or what-ever, more engagement.' However, her feed did not grow as much as she'd hoped, so Rose opted for a shortcut and paid for fake followers sent by booster pages where she spent up to $20 per shout-out. Each one grew her page up to 2,000 followers, but these were mostly spam accounts rather than the devoted and lucrative community of young women she aspired to.

'I paid for like one or two shout-outs,' she recounts, 'but you can pay like $50. It just depends how desperate you are.' The main problem with paying for shout-outs is that it sends a signal to the internet's most nefarious operators that you are exactly that: desperate. Desperate to be someone or desperately in need of a pay cheque. Desperate aspiration is the internet's most exploitable commodity, and buying a shout-out is the online equivalent of sparking a light bulb in a pitch-black field of blood-sucking insects.

One of the many internet users to find Rose was a woman she came to call Alisha. A representative from a shiny American network marketing conglomerate called It Works!, Alisha offered Rose opportunities online for sisterhood and success. 'She found me on Instagram,' says Rose, 'and I really liked her energy.' She accepted an invitation to join Alisha's private group, the 'boss tribe': mostly young women, single mothers and housewives short of money. 'There were a lot of mums, women with families. Then there were women even in their fifties and just looking for a career change.' Alisha and the women in the group shared positive and faux-feminist empowerment messages with each other about overcoming the odds. This resonated with Rose, who was in need of hope. The main messages from Alisha were more direct: 'Join It Works!' and 'Be Your Own Boss'.

The company promised an army of young women the chance to earn a good living selling mid-range health products both offline to family and friends and to strangers on social media. Each recruit would not technically be employed by the company; instead they would become a self-employed 'distributor', with the status to sell through a code and therefore the ability to earn commissions on sales based on their volume. There was no hourly wage or salary. The company motto stated that you 'earn the income you deserve'.

Founded by a Midwestern entrepreneur called Michael Pentecost at the turn of the millennium, It Works! was built in the mould of both an evangelist church and a summer club. The company puts on mega-conferences with inspirational speakers, music and light shows for paying attendees, who are the same people tasked with selling its products. The mini-concerts inspire the workforce to stay part of the It Works! family, but it's a family you have to pay to join. In 2001, the company was making a loss, but as the world's attention migrated online, Pentecost cracked the key to sales and declared revenues of over $1.2bn and a global workforce of more than 60,000.[2]

Pentecost proudly parades his riches online. The company website features pictures of his ranch and mansion situated on his private island. The company passed on one message to its recruits above all others: if you work hard, you too can be as successful as Mike. 'Never Stop Dreaming' was another of their straplines.

For Rose, It Works! had a certain glamour. 'They're an American-based company so they have people from all around the world. It was also super cool because I've always wanted to go to America. They have conferences and all sorts.' The company is reliant on finding new people to recruit, and the promise of self-sufficiency led Rose to join. 'I was just going with whatever opportunities were gonna come my way, because for me it became about survival, financial survival.'

However, rather than ensuring her financial survival, It Works! did the opposite. Each month the company deducts a series of non-negotiable fees from its distributors. It charges its sellers a joining fee of $99 and an additional $30 a month to access their own seller's page on the company website. It also requires an automatic subscription of between $99 and $589 a month for new products. Rose estimated her monthly costs at $180. The problem was she was making nothing. 'I had an auto shipment [payment] try to come out of my account and I couldn't afford to pay it because of my financial circumstances.' Her finances were so dire, she was being pursued by debt collectors.

She blamed herself for her failure to make money, but this was because she didn't realise she was not the salesman; she was the customer. According to the income disclosure statement the company released in 2019, 85.94 per cent of its distributors made less than $1.60 a day.[3] Most were like Rose and made nothing at all. Not one person signed up as a distributor earned more than the US median income of $68,703,[4] despite the promises of immense wealth and the enormous revenues the company generated for its founder. It Works! made its money signing up young women and keeping them paying into the platform as long as possible even as they took home nothing. Many who had signed up were oblivious to the hustle, only to realise later that they had been scammed. They now bombard internet review sites with warnings and complaints. 'This is a scam and a pyramid scheme,'[5] said one former distributor who had paid into the company for a year.

Unbeknown to Rose, It Works! had long been accused of 'preying on directionless millennials and single moms'.[6] It had incentivised young women to auto-enrol into large monthly payments with the promise of earning a higher commission earlier. In reality, the only way they could make anything was to recruit their friends and family or enlist other young women facing precarity in the workplace.

The model of affiliate marketing the company uses is part of an old tradition to which the internet has given a new life and a million different masks. There are more businesses like It Works! than can be counted, and they are exploiting millions under the guise of offering young women empowerment in the age of get-rich feminism. Avon and Herbalife are the biggest names to have made this model of direct selling famous, but now it has become infamous with a host of scandals involving newer outfits.

The California-based company LuLaRoe promised young women the chance to be entrepreneurs by directly selling its colourful line of cheaply produced womenswear, such as its signature fluorescent leggings. It became an over-night success, signing up housewives to hawk for it under the title of 'consultant'. The average initial deposit from each woman who joined was $5,000.[7] There was also a rigorous incentive structure that encouraged women to sign up other sellers beneath them.

The women at the top were given a cut of all the orders below them. Some early joiners registered monthly incomes of up to $40,000, raised from thousands of other women. Sales of the colourful leggings were not bad either, although a disclosure statement by the company revealed that the real median bonus payment earned by consultants during its boom in 2016 was just $526 per year, or $1.20 a day.[8] As such, it is easy to see why consultants were pressed on the importance of recruitment. That was where the real money was made. 'You sign people up in a way to move up the fastest,' said one consultant, speaking to the business publication *Bloomberg*. Each level unlocked different rewards. Recruitment was known as 'stacking' – a term ironically also used in hip-hop for making money. Overnight the company did just that. Within five years of being launched in 2012, LuLaRoe was posting revenue of over $2bn.[9]

The company pressured its consultants to put all the money they made back into buying new stock. The founders reprimanded consultants who complained when they struggled to sell the supplies they had bought, calling the women 'stale' and demanding they go and find new customers.[10] As the company boomed, it also began to struggle with the production pressures. Consultants began to find the clothes they had ordered were damaged, contaminated or not fit for purpose. The company introduced a policy promising to refund any unsold clothing, but when consultants tried to demand refunds en masse, many found it impossible to access any kind of compensation. Some women realised they were sitting on as much as $40,000 worth of clothing that no one wanted to buy and were financially ruined. As with other pyramid schemes, you could only sell to and sign up so many women in your neighbourhood without the supply of people you knew eventually running out.

In the US, companies like LuLaRoe and It Works! are allowed to deploy hierarchical multi-level marketing models if they can argue that the main goal is to sell products.

However, models like this become a scam when their goal is to trick consumers into buying inventory regardless of whether they sell it, and thousands of LuLaRoe's estimated 150,000 sellers were claiming that the company was doing exactly that. The company has been publicly condemned as a pyramid scheme and a scam in several class-action lawsuits taken out by former sellers.[11] In 2021, it paid out $4.75m to settle a consumer protection suit, although it continued to deny wrongdoing.[12]

The pyramids – the wonder of the digital world

The gig economy has replaced twentieth-century expectations of fair pay and workers' rights with an emphasis on individual enterprise and a promise of flexibility. However, whereas Uber, the poster child of the gig economy, is often called exploitative, it is not an outright con, unlike the thousands of scam companies using the rules of the gig economy to manipulate workers displaced by an economic consensus that says they are on their own.

Bloomberg reported that the number of Americans participating in direct selling had grown from 15.6 million in 2011 to 20.5 million in 2016.[13] Three quarters of those were women, often young mothers trying to make ends meet in a country without statutory maternity pay. If, like me, you grew up in an underprivileged area, your Facebook feed is likely to be littered with posts from old school friends inviting you to 'make money from home, DM me to find out how'. Pyramid schemes are not only booming; they are becoming the default business model of the social media age: a model that turns follower hierarchies into income streams and allows individuals to monetise their personal relationships, turning friends into followers for the benefit of phantom companies that leech off the unwaged or underemployed.

It Works! was not the only company to reach out to Rose. Other businesses messaged her daily. 'They leave comments on my pictures and they can be quite pushy. "Please DM me, we've got a request for you, we think you're amazing, we think you'd be fabulous for our company." I delete them or I don't answer back ... but some of them I am interested in and I will answer and I will contact. I like to say yes to opportunities,' she tells me, though she is unsure which offers conceal a trick and which a treat. Rose also had a desire to be seen as something other than 'mental'. Her marketing work gave her validation as a businesswoman. However, although she shouted out products that were her 'vibe' to get brands' attention, more often than not they had approached her first despite her relatively low number of followers.

In an age when the power of 'pass it on' can generate billions, anyone can exert influence online. Overnight, companies have realised they can do this without it costing them a penny by capitalising on the desire for micro-celebrity. For example, one of the many companies to reach out to Rose was a so-called beach jewellery brand named Palmpe. The company uses a Gmail address as its primary business account but still manages to convince thousands of young women every month to become ambassadors for the brand.

At first glance, the company's model is far less nefarious than LuLaRoe or It Works!. It sends direct messages (DMs) to thousands of young women with a few hundred followers or more who are hoping to become influencers. Its 'ambassadors programme' promises free jewellery, and all these lucky influencers have to do is pay for the postage and packaging. Rose was told she could visit the website and select an item, then a special code would grant her a 100 per cent discount. She went onto the website and ordered. The items on display ranged from $16 to $260. After a challenging year, she felt she was living the dream. She was an ambassador for a youthful brand and receiving free jewellery. She was a step closer to making a living online. But as always, there was a catch.

Palmpe presents itself as an exclusive jewellery company, but in fact its items can be purchased on the budget Chinese retail site Alibaba for cents. The $20 posting and packaging is 66 times the actual value of the item and is how the company actually generates income. Palmpe is a dropshipping company using the game-changing shopping software Shopify, which allows orders to be made directly from manufacturers in China. In other words, it is just an Instagram account and a website.

Palmpe may not be running a pyramid scheme, but the endless new phantom companies like it are still exploiting those in pursuit of the influencer gold rush. Their 'ambassadors' believe they are helping to sell the brand, but in reality they are its buyers. Online I have met many aspiring influencers who started out desperate to hack the secret of success only to end up being scammed. One was even taken in by a US president.

The birth of a saleswoman

Tarla Makaeff makes YouTube tutorials that hardly anybody watches and sets internet challenges that hardly anybody accepts. Her selfies are airbrushed with Facetune, a photo editing app popular with college girls, and she can be found on TikTok, Triller or any of the video-making apps frequented by teenagers. The forty-something Californian lives online like a 17-year-old but offline has had more lives than a feline. She has been an actor, a model, a Pilates instructor and a copywriter, to name just a few of her many hats. Her latest reinvention is as an internet guru for hire and the head honcho of her so-called 'boss babes' society, a group for entrepreneurial women. Tarla promises millennials that she can launch their careers as influencers and internet entrepreneurs if they pay her.

The US is a nation of salesmen. The success of early-twentieth-century American manufacturing is owed to buccaneering marketers and ambitious consumers trying to sell and buy their way up the social ladder. At the dawn of America's consumer society the door-to-door salesman was omnipresent. Today, the travelling pedlar does not even need to leave the house. The new salesmen sell get-rich-quick workshops over WhatsApp and promise to show you how to make money from your smartphone. They sell confidence packaged as expertise, a product that is free to manufacture and has an infinite mark-up. The American essayist Jia Tolentino wrote that 'the con is in the DNA of this country, which was founded on the idea that it is good, important, and even noble to see an opportunity to profit and take whatever you can. The story is as old as the first Thanksgiving.'[14]

America still reveres and recites the country's first con. The US Constitution elevated and enshrined the importance of civil rights at a time when most of the nation had none. Native Americans, women and enslaved Africans could not vote or own property. Today, all those marginalized groups are invited to have a seat at the table and a shot at capitalism, even though the men long seated are already fat with their gains. Today's confidence salesmen are influencers, exaggerators, scammers and celebrity entrepreneurs. The most belligerent and boisterous of recent times is Donald J. Trump, the influencer who became president. The billionaire real estate magnate changed Tarla's life when she enrolled at his 'university' for aspiring entrepreneurs. Trump University promised to teach its founder's 'real estate secrets' and allocate hand-picked mentors offering around-the-clock consultancy. What Tarla actually learnt from the course was that she, along with thousands of other students, had been duped.

Trump University was the embodiment of a businessman who makes money selling his name rather than building companies. It was supposed to offer educational services for budding real estate moguls and entrepreneurs, but in reality it was a cash cow designed to compete in the murky world of get-rich-quick speaker seminars that make their money selling bogus workshops. The instructors were high-pressure salesmen paid a commission of 25 per cent to up-sell consumers onto even more expensive courses.[15] There was a free seminar designed to sign people up to a $1,495 course, which was itself designed to persuade students to take the supposed elite course costing $35,000.[16] If they did not have the money, they were encouraged to use their credit cards, which for some would mean an eye-watering final bill of up to $87,000. To make matters worse, students accused speakers and mentors of financial exploitation. There were allegations of mentors taking out loans in their students' names,[17] and even coercing them into deals in which those mentors had a vested interest. The best summary of Trump University is from the affidavit of Ronald Schnackenberg, the man whose job it was to sell it: 'Based upon my personal experience and employment, I believe that Trump University was a fraudulent scheme, and that it preyed upon the elderly and uneducated to separate them from their money.'[18] One of the thousands scammed was Tarla Makaeff.

Unlike the thousands of young extroverts who descend on Los Angeles every year hoping to become famous, Tarla was born and raised in the city but had none of the flamboyance. 'I was a bit of an introvert, I got bullied as a child,' she told me. She describes her upbringing as middle class but not without challenges. Her father died in an accident shortly after she was born and her French-Canadian mother gave up full-time work with the support of the compensation payout. After high school, like many Californians blessed with youth and good looks in the 1990s, Tarla was absorbed into Hollywood.

Despite being painfully shy, she recalls being an extra in the Julia Roberts blockbuster *My Best Friend's Wedding*, a hand double in the daytime TV drama *Diagnosis: Murder* and a body stand-in on *Beverly Hills, 90210*. She was even hired to provide 'aesthetic ambience'. 'There were games with the Clippers and stuff and they would hire girls who were models to literally decorate the place, be decor, hang out, that was literally the point of an ambience model.' In other words, Tarla was a hottie for hire.

However, being young and beautiful only lasts for so long in an industry with a high turnover of human flesh. By a stroke of luck, Tarla ended up working in copywriting, first as an underpaid employee, then as a high-earning freelancer. At one stage she was clearing $20,000 a month, until her only client's restructuring collapsed her income to zero. Her woes were compounded when her mother became ill. 'I didn't have a husband, I didn't have a second income, so I'm in the midst of all this, my work's winding down, my mum's having a heart attack and then I'm stressed about my house and that's kind of how the whole Trump thing came into all of this.'

It's easier to work out what Trump has not put his name to than what he has. There has been Trump Ice, Trump Shuttle and Trump Mortgage, to name just a few. All failed in typical fashion: they over-promised, under-delivered and were engulfed in allegations of misrepresentation. Trump University was no different. Leading instructors were reportedly paid up to $25,000 to make motivational sales pitches such as 'you came here because you want to improve your life' or 'if you want to feel like a loser then go home, if you want to feel like a winner then sign on the bottom line, the money will come back to you'. These were both sentiments I'd heard in my mother's evangelical church. The top salesman, James Harris, had a reported conversion rate of 25 per cent, which means that in a room of 1,000 people, he was able to single-handedly generate Trump University $8,750,000.[19]

Most of the salesmen masquerading as instructors came via a man named Mark Dove, described by former employee Stephen Gilpin as 'the ringmaster in the world of front end, high pressure speaker scams'.[20] Despite the claim that Trump would hand-pick the speakers, it appeared that nobody senior did due diligence on mentors.[21] According to Gilpin, students were taught 'highly speculative' strategies, while instructors breached laws designed to protect consumers against being scammed and encouraged students to act illegally. They even encouraged students to invest in dubious plans, including Ponzi schemes. According to Schnackenberg, 'the primary goal of Trump University was not to educate students regarding real estate investing. The primary focus seemed to be to make money as quickly and easily as possible.'

Tarla only realised something was wrong when it was too late.[22] 'I didn't intend to invest any money. I was kind of shocked because it was a three-day seminar. I paid the $750 and then at the end they did this huge up-sell for a $35,000 programme. That's not normally something I would ever do but I was in a desperate and a vulnerable position and I was thinking that this could help me basically get back to a six-figure or multiple six-figure income which I basically no longer had.' She could not afford the fees so was encouraged to charge them to her credit card. Like all students on the elite package, she was promised in-the-field support and analysis on deals, but this advice was often against her interests. She was misquoted property valuations on deals that would have resulted in substantial losses. She alleges that when she changed her mind, real estate documents were signed in her name by somebody else. Soon other students alleged that mentors had fraudulently procured credit in their names too.

Schnackenberg claims he did not see Trump once in his time working at Trump University, suggesting the billionaire barely contributed to the programme, but even if he had, how different would it have been? The company was following Trump's get-rich-or-lie-trying philosophy perfectly.

Tarla eventually turned to a lawyer, and led a class-action lawsuit against the man soon to be elected president. Trump sued her in retaliation, pushing her to the brink of suicide, but Tarla kept fighting and won the only way David might beat Goliath in America – in a court settlement. Trump had promised he would never compromise, but days before the case was due to be heard, he gave in and a staggering $25m settlement was agreed, to be shared between all the claimants.[23] Tarla considers the victory to be the most heroic event of her life. However, despite beating Trump, she then went on to do something surprising: she turned into him.

The settlement with Trump was a huge relief, but it did not solve all Tarla's problems. She had sold her home, her mother had died, and Donald J. Trump had even been elected president. Without work, she felt the lack of direction that had marked her early twenties, but without the youth. She was starting again in the years when she'd expected to be settled, and pursued random careers including a brief interlude as a Pilates instructor working at high-end gyms like Equinox. 'I basically was out of the workforce for quite a while, so it was really hard to return to anything.' She was alone and drifting towards her fifties. 'Those kind of feel like your last years to like meet someone, get married and have kids, and so …' She tails off.

In her early twenties she had been a model of sorts, and now she tried her hand at it again. She no longer suited the casting calls for ambience modelling but found there was good but irregular money to be made as a fitting model – models that clothing companies tested sizes on. It helped her to pay her bills but it was hardly a career, and so she kept looking for something more lucrative. Then she saw the Facebook post of an old high school friend, who was offering an opportunity to make good money.

When Tarla replied to the post, she did not realise that she was about to tumble back into a world of predatory businesses exploiting consumer naïvety. It was an invitation to join a multi-level marketing company (MLM) offering riches by signing up every last friend on Facebook to the scheme. Tarla fell for it and then down a rabbit hole from one scheme into another. When one appeared to fail, she would try a new scheme selling something different. 'One was jewellery-based, one was skincare-based, one was wine-based. It was like the syndrome that I see from a lot of other people that are in that network marketing space: if it's not working in one company, they'll jump to the next.' Once you enter the world of MLMs, it's hard to leave. The model is part-business and part-family, but if you dare to stop paying your dues, you're dead to everyone still in the racket, because you effectively pay for their friendship. Each MLM is structured like a church or even a cult.

As time went on, Tarla transformed herself into an internet micro-influencer and marketing guru, with a new YouTube channel and business Facebook page. She posted videos about how to successfully sign people up to MLMs using elementary psychological mind games not dissimilar from those employed at Trump University. She told members that the way to sell to someone was to pretend that you were not, adding that you asked a prospective recruit, 'Do you know anyone who would be interested?' as if the opportunity was not for them. 'What it does is it's like telling a child you can't have that candy and then the child wants it more,' she said. 'It kind of gets them off their guard.' She even claimed that she tried to sign up her doctor, and encouraged followers to show ambition with their recruiting to find committed buyers. She used high-pressure selling, but she drew the line at encouraging recruits and members to take on debt and instead recommended they make the money to cover joining fees by having a 'garage sale'. She also told people, 'It can be free to join if you enrol three customers.'

In her regular videos, Tarla jumped from fad to fad, waxing lyrical about Bitcoin opportunities and encouraging friends to invest their money. The videos gave an impression of success, but offline she was barely getting by. 'I wasn't making any money with the network marketing, of course. I made some money but it wasn't good money.' In network marketing parlance, if you are not making good money, you are probably losing it, and so she went back to the drawing board, dropping the MLMs but keeping the new influencer persona. 'Subscribe to my channel to get more information on how to make money online,' she posted, despite being unable to do so herself.

She would comment all day on the pages of strangers to build engagement, paying for ads and using hashtags prolifically. The views on most of her YouTube videos barely entered double figures, let alone the hundreds or thousands. She often looked out of place online but persisted until she found a shortcut. She installed the bot ManyChat on Facebook, which in her words 'spread like wildfire'. Chatbots engage in multiple conversations at once with strangers to drive engagement and traffic. How meaningful the connections made are is questionable, but the sheer volume means you can boost your follower numbers. 'There were literally 260,000 on my chatbot. I'm not kidding. Obviously it's not all targeted people and I don't even know how it was growing.'

Although Tarla managed to grow her Facebook business page to 100,000 followers by paying for traffic, the vast majority were not organic or engaged; many were bots or digital marketers themselves, meaning today no one comments on most of her posts. The manoeuvre was also seen as dishonest spamming by Facebook and led to her account being temporarily suspended. Despite the short-term loss, however, her tactics paid off. In her mid forties she had managed to build what looked like a considerable online audience. Social media experts consider followers inflated by notorious techniques to be a kind of fraud when influencers attempt to trade off enhanced numbers, but either way Tarla now looked impressive and was planning to sell digital workshops for up to $1,000 on how to build a social media following and launch an influencer career, using herself as an example of success.

She adopted an online persona that felt as manufactured as her following. The middle-aged white Californian litters her posts with phrases like 'hey boo' and 'I got you girl' appropriated from African-American women. On her website she tells visitors to 'get ready to hustle your way to freedom through free marketing strategies that attract drool-worthy clients', and 'Learn social media marketing and online marketing like yesterday? I so get it, girlfran'.' She has also self-published a book, *The Essential Guide to Online Marketing*. She describes her target audience as working women between 25 and 45 who want to quit their jobs to be affluent entrepreneurs. In other words, her target is women like her – or, as she calls them, 'Boss Babes'.

Tarla launched her Boss Babes Society at the start of 2020. It's a group with a familiar premise. Female empowerment has become a billion-dollar industry as more young women graduate from top universities, occupy more top jobs and aspire not to marry a wealthy partner but to become one themselves. A whole industry of speakers, awards and events has popped up promising to inspire and equip ambitious young women to reap the rewards of capitalism while often only empowering the women at the top who are raking in the cash from speaking and sponsorship.

There was nothing original about Tarla's society. Even the name had been copied to death. Boss Babe Inc., which launched years earlier, runs a so-called 12-week 'Instagram growth accelerator', a course it says will show young women how to grow and make money from Instagram for the cool price of $2,297.[24] The company, founded by two glamorous and heavily filtered British Instagram influencers living in Los Angeles, now has an online following of over three million. At the time of writing, Tarla's Boss Babes Facebook group, which is built around elevating her status as an internet guru, has only 68 followers, and at least three of them are accounts run by Tarla herself. Very few recent posts on it have any engagement.

When I ask Tarla what qualifies her to be an expert influencer, beyond her repeated failures, she becomes coy and defensive. 'I mean look, we could argue. I think they say to be an expert at something you need to have 10,000 hours. I have to go back and see how many hours I have over the last couple of years, right probably not that many but I definitely consider myself to be getting close to expert status if I'm not already. I really know everything that you need to do,' she tells me. When I ask her how much money she makes online, I get a similar reply, but she concedes she is not making a lot. It's unclear if she is even making the minimum wage. 'Well I'm still in the building-up phase of my business but I made some money, not tons, from the network marketing and the affiliate marketing.' Despite this, she believes she is qualified to target young women with her $1,000 digital influencer course. 'I'm giving them the whole game plan including the end plan because when you come online a big part of the problem is it's this shrouded mystery, "How do you really make money online, how are these people doing it?" and I really feel like nobody wants to tell you.' In actual fact, everybody does, for a fee, even if they have no idea.

The global online professional education market is estimated to be worth $280bn.[25] Although much of it is made up of accredited elite business courses, the demand from ordinary working people trying to improve their options is being met by an ever-growing pool of charlatans or self-professed experts. It's understandable why the demand for their services is on the rise, as technology makes the future of work appear precarious, whilst the cost of living and the pressure to live in luxury increase. The self-development industry, with its low barriers of entry, has drawn in those without a clear trade. Many businesses have start-up costs, but all you need to be a guru is a smartphone and a website. Anyone can search for elementary information online, rewrite it and repackage themselves as an expert. There are business coaches with no experience of business and life coaches with limited experience of life.

Some people overtly admit to faking it till they make it. The space is filled with millennials, but also older people in transition like Tarla. Whether these internet gurus can offer value or even do what they promise is an afterthought. The only thing that matters is whether there is a market for their service, whether people believe they are who they say and can deliver what they are selling. It is the ease of profiting from our desire to improve that led Donald Trump to license his name to the Trump University scam, and it was financial desperation that led to Tarla losing $35,000.

There is a glaring irony to Tarla's reinvention. She was scammed by a course taught by unqualified teachers promising to reveal the 'secrets of real estate' but with no experience of what they claimed. Today, she is presenting herself as a social media guru running a course she claims can help you to launch a career as an influencer or digital entrepreneur, having spent most of her time online failing to do just that. She is not the only one running this hustle, although unlike Trump, what motivates Tarla is ambition rather than greed.

We are all tempted to overplay our expertise to maximise our opportunities, but in the influencer economy this is happening on an industrial scale. Tarla does have a copywriting background, but her internet community was engineered, and those she spoke to regularly online were often internet users doing the same thing as her: pretending to be friends in the hope that they might drive a sale. Friendship has always been a part of business, but in the past, the space between the personal and the professional was more clearly defined. Today, friends are converted into followers and followers into communities built by the cult of a carefully manufactured personality. Tarla, who grew up shy in the suburbs, was now a confident, urbane internet expert and a bold American saleswoman. She had gone from being scammed by Donald Trump to running his playbook, a manual for the entire attention economy.

6

THE ART OF THE HACK

In recent years, scrolling my social media timeline has become an aggressive game of dodgeball. Each day I shimmy past a never-ending feed of pyramid schemes, scams, network marketers and self-promoters making 'motivational' posts preaching that there is no excuse for being poor in the age of social media aimed at aspirational working-class internet users. A common one says: 'If you are not from a rich family, a rich family must come from you.' The infatuation with hustle has veered from the extreme to the ridiculous. A now infamous viral post from a wannabe hustler proudly boasted that if he had to choose between dinner with a billionaire and a cash deposit of $1m, the dinner would be more useful in helping him to become a millionaire than the million dollars itself. Twitter may have laughed, but this desire to be self-made is so pervasive that even having a well-paid job is regularly derided as selling yourself short. After all, if you're not trying to join the 1 per cent, then what are you doing with your life?

The extreme values of the hustler spirit play out on every platform. In numerous groups on the audio app Clubhouse there are regular debates that painfully consider whether 'broke men deserve love'. According to hustle law, sex should be a privilege of the affluent and the successful. In one conversation, a 20-year-old student with a part-time job who lived at home earnestly asked if he should be allowed to date women or if that required him to get 'his money up'. The seemingly jovial topic has gone viral, but as I watch it pop up more regularly than the bus I take to work, I read more and more responses from those on low incomes suggesting that a small bank balance is a character flaw.

It is unsurprising that in this climate there has emerged an insatiable desire to be wealthy and an unending supply of so-called advice on how. On the internet there are over 1.3 billion entries when you search 'how to get rich'. On YouTube the videos claiming to show you 'how to become wealthy on a low income' or 'how to make $1,000 a day from your smartphone' have total views in the hundreds of millions. Each video is a rabbit hole to a new scheme. One of the most popular is dropshipping, which allows you to run an ecommerce business without ever handling the product you are selling.

The dropshipping phenomenon has boomed with the availability of easy-to-use, low-cost software that allows you to set up an online shop without a business operation or having to touch a product. To dropship you do not even need to talk to a supplier; instead you act as a middleman, selling products that are listed on Chinese online retail services like AliExpress. It is an industry emblematic of our age of shortcuts: the software does the work so you don't have to. The only thing necessary is to build a brand that looks the part, which is easier than ever before. High-functioning and professional-looking websites are now simple to self-build using cheap templates from DIY web design companies like Squarespace, whose own motto is 'A website makes it real'.

If Squarespace makes it easy to look legitimate online, it is Shopify that makes the dropship life possible. Your customer places an order from your online Shopify store; the software automatically sends the order to your dropshipping supplier; your dropshipping supplier prepares the order and ships it directly to the customer. Shopify makes the process dummy-proof. You pick a theme, an app connects directly to suppliers you will never meet, and you upload the pictures of what you are selling. These are often ripped from the websites and social media videos of competitors, and then the key trick is to run adverts on sites like Facebook.

Between 2014 and 2018, Facebook's algorithms were designed to send videos, pictures and posts viral, leading influencers flocking to the site to grow their platforms. They were not the only ones. When I joined in my first year of university, Facebook was a site where you only saw posts from your friends, but in recent years, hustlers of every hue have bombarded it with efforts to game the algorithm so that you see more of the hidden adverts for whatever product they are dropshipping. Facebook admits to difficulties freeing the site of spam,[1] despite changing their algorithms. In some cases marketers have deployed nefarious techniques that breach Facebook's rules through manipulation, deception, unethical decisions and even scams. Gaming or 'black-hat hacking' has become part and parcel of the strategy of the digital hustlers running behind the so-called 'drop shoppers' craze.

On Shopify you can make easy money without the risk attached to stocking products and running a full business operation. The technology can even find the suppliers; all you have to do is choose which items to market. For just $29 a month, you can create a shop on the world's leading ecommerce site builder. Since 2012, over a million[2] internet users across the world have signed up to the platform. Few have been more successful than Joel Contartese, a digital hustler who has turned black-hat marketing into an art form and has mastered making money from influencers without being one himself.

California dreamin'

I found the Argentinian-American through a *Forbes* magazine profile in which he was hailed as a pioneer of influencer marketing. I arranged to meet him at the Montage in Beverly Hills, a luxury hotel built in the style of a Spanish colonial garrison. The palatial estate sits in the world's most glamorous triangle, one block down from LA's Rodeo Drive, a road synonymous with fame and fortune, where the flagship stores of high-end brands stand like places of worship. On this block the poor and even the middle classes are unworthy and impure. Rooms at the Montage start from $850 a night.

When Joel arrived in the imposing lobby, he shook my hand and sat down opposite me, at home in his polo shirt and smart trainers. He liked to bring guests to the Montage, he told me, as it gave off the right impression. The 28-year-old was well-spoken, with a light Latin American accent, and had become a rare winner in the den of internet thieves. Although he had been featured in business magazines as a whiz-kid of the influencer economy, his real skill was in digital subterfuge, with the help of hacks.

Joel's life started over 6,000 miles away, in Argentina, as the first son of a 'very prominent business owner'. He described his early years as plentiful until the 1998 banking crisis hit Latin America and left Argentina facing a crippling financial crisis. When the country's economy collapsed, Joel's parents lost everything: 'All their savings. All their properties. Everything. So at that point they had to make a decision and they felt that it would be best for our futures, me and my brothers, to go to a country with more opportunity.'

The family headed to America, and coincidentally settled in the same part of Florida as my grandparents. However, the success his parents had achieved in Argentina evaded them in the so-called land of opportunity. They were outsiders. Joel's father, now aged 73, was still working when I met Joel. 'You know: they didn't know the language, they didn't know people, they came at an older age and because of different circumstances they never had a chance to get to the top of their game … We grew up in a household here in the States where I always had everything that I needed but never more. Rent was a struggle at times, we were homeless once or twice, not for long periods, I'm talking about a few days.'

For the children of migrants, education is often the primary path to social mobility, but Joel was not academic; he was street smart. After high school, he tried Broward College, but dropped out to throw himself into entrepreneurial pursuits. He quickly found that he intuitively understood the burgeoning internet language of 'memes'. Online, we litter our communication with emojis and pictures. Sometimes we use photos we have taken ourselves;

others are amateur pictures that have gone viral, but many are directly cut from pop culture media, such as Disney cartoons or Hollywood films. These memes are the most widely shared media in the world. They are tweeted, forwarded and reposted. They go viral daily. Little bits of culture and banter that can be anything from insider jokes on niche topics to mainstream satire.

A viral meme used to be as ephemeral as a newspaper headline, but that was until kids started collecting them by creating pages on Facebook and Instagram, known as meme accounts, reposting the funniest ones that related to their subculture, their community or a key theme. Initially, the aim was to make as many people laugh as possible.

In 2012, a few years after Instagram was launched, Joel's friend Joseph reached out about creating meme accounts. The idea sounded cool, and lots of other young people were already doing it too. Joseph downloaded Instagram and set up their first accounts, scouring social media for the most viral memes. Within a few short years they had grown a handful of feeds with millions of followers. 'We grew five accounts. We had 12 million followers,' Joel said. He was barely 20. As early adopters, many of the accounts they set up also had names that made them easy to find, like @ipostvids.

'We had a parody account called @FerellWill, we had @giftedvoices, which came in down the line. We had

@opticalillusions, which was an account dedicated to posting cool memes where it looks like one thing but it's another. Once video was [popular], we had one of the first Latin-themed Instagrams, @bestvinesLatino. We were taking Hispanic themes, Vines, and posting it on Instagram, and we grew a huge audience of Latin followers.'

Joel and Joseph were not creating any of the jokes, images or videos. They merely saw the things people shared and reposted them on a single Instagram page as part of a practice known as curation. They were among thousands of teenagers and young adults across the world accruing large amounts of attention merely because they posted memes in one place. Unbeknown to them, this would make them serious money.

After the follower numbers on their themed pages boomed, Joel says he and Joseph began fielding enquiries from companies asking them to covertly promote products. 'We had 12 million followers. We were approached a few months later by a supplements company called Shredz to do paid advertisements on our pages, and so it kind of sparked the idea that we could monetise this hobby that we created ... We could reach out to similar brands across Instagram and even local businesses and we started to sell ad spots on our page.' In 2012, most themed pages appeared advertisement-free. Today, they are paid to promote everything from ride-hailing apps like Uber to gambling companies with ads disguised as memes (often in breach of advertising guidelines).

Shredz would change everything for Joel. The company, which sold weight-loss and bodybuilding supplements, was an early adopter of the influencer business model and also the obsessive body-image culture of Instagram, rife with six-packs and pouting. Not only did they want to take out paid ads on Joel's themed pages; they also offered him an actual job in New Jersey, with a salary. He accepted, but leaving home to take the role meant he missed out on a lucrative payday from the themed meme pages he had built with Joseph. 'There was no equity or agreement in place. It was kind of like two friends from high school who were doing this thing, you know. I went off to do something else and he continued to do that. He has sold accounts and he made $100,000 selling those accounts but he still has a few that he runs himself,' Joel said. 'I left in 2013 to do my own thing. I can't come back seven years later and ask for a cut.'

When Joel got to New Jersey, he was faced with adulthood for the first time. Until then, he had never even done his own laundry. He was a momma's boy now working in Shredz's corporate sweatshop, albeit with a salary that made him the highest earner in his family at just 22 years old.

Shredz had been founded by an enterprising young influencer, Arvin Lal, who was only a few years older than

Joel himself. The median age of the employees was 25, and Joel estimated that of the 60-odd workers, he was one of the youngest. The company housed its core workers in a warehouse in Jersey, and every day he worked multiple shifts. 'We worked 9 a.m. to 6 p.m. and then we could come back at 9 p.m. and work until midnight. The company paid for our housing a mile and a half from the office and they kept everyone in these apartment complexes so there was no excuse for anyone to not go to work or not get there on time.' Joel's job consisted of paying themed accounts to post covert ads disguised as memes with captions that told their page followers to follow Shredz in what were called shout-outs.

'We focused heavily on the themed account, very similar to what I owned previously, and we were spending like $200,000 a week … We were giving them clickbaity viral content and all the content was, kind of like a snippet, "find out how to lose back fat" or "learn how to detox your body, follow Shredz supplements for more", so we were always using these accounts, redirecting eyeballs onto our Instagram page … then we started to [enlist] micro-influencers or athletes and what I mean by athletes is we were looking for people who were just fit on Instagram.'

Shredz's claim that it had helped hundreds of thousands of people 'take control of their lives and become something they've always aspired to be' may have been dubious, but it

THE ART OF THE HACK

proved to be successful. The company's supplements were being sold by a growing proliferation of super-fit gym trainers and models who found a natural home on Instagram, setting their followers 30-day get-fit challenges and telling them that Shredz could help them improve their looks. The company incentivised Instagram micro-influencers to post gym selfies and topless training photographs using hashtags like #Shredz and #ShredzArmy. At last count there have been almost five million such posts made.

However, the company became embroiled in controversy[3] as it emerged that some of its key 'athletes' were editing their pictures to look more enhanced, using software like Photoshop.[4] In some cases they had even had cosmetic procedures while attributing their bodies to hard work in the gym and a diet of Shredz. The people selling the products were outed as frauds, but even if they had not broken any law, they had written new ones, which were being followed by a generation of Instagram users. Companies like Shredz have channelled millions of dollars into challenging millennials to have the perfect body, and helped to saturate Instagram with images of unattainable body goals. Joel says Shredz invented the template that has now become ubiquitous among companies trading online on our insecurities. 'We were the first to really do it,' he claims.

Shredz provided an education for Joel. He learnt how to scout effective influencers, how to buy adverts on social media platforms, and a range of nefarious black-hat marketing tricks that made his boss rich. He could see how the new gold rush rewarded the brave and he wanted to be a player rather than an employee. So he handed in his notice and bought himself a one-way plane ticket to California. 'When you think about trends, LA, California, but more specifically LA is where you want to be,' he told me, reclining under a ray of sunshine. Since swapping the East Coast for the West, he has reaped the benefits of his gamble, but he had a few stumbles along the way. He married a woman he wooed on Twitter and reunited with his old friend from Florida, Joseph, who also relocated. Together they launched a bunch of failed ventures, from clones of Shredz to a marketing consultancy agency.

'A lot of other people are gonna wanna shut down after that, but not me. It hurts me and for a day or two I feel like damn, but then I get back up and try again.' Joel reminds me of the cartoon lab mice from the animated television series *Pinky and the Brain*. Pinky would ask his scheming friend 'What do you want to do tonight?' and Brain's stock reply would always be: 'Same thing we do every night, try to take over the world.' Joel's resolve to make millions only strengthened as venture after venture foundered, until his breakthrough came in the murky world of internet dropshipping.

How to hack Facebook

In 2017, Joel launched the website Shopolis with Joseph. The shopping site had a blue logo and an online presence that was branded like Amazon. Joel used both paid ads on Facebook and stealthily hidden advertisements to build up huge traction for the random products they were selling from the warehouses of suppliers in China, stocking anything from a teacup that stirred itself to mini-helicopters. 'It was just very gimmicky products like a pancake flipper. As a matter of fact Kylie Jenner used it on her Instagram story one time. It's like a red circle that goes on a pan and it has other circles inside made from like silicon,' Joel describes. A buyer makes pancake mix separately and 'so you pour it all over and you flip and you make five pancakes at the same time. It's gimmicky … It's stupid little products like that [but] you're moving 10,000 products a day. You're making a ton of money.'

He always kept an eye out for opportunities to expand sales. Facebook and Google are so dominant in internet commerce that shifting products has moved from an art into a science. The price paid to the big platforms for a click that guarantees traffic is set. But Shopolis also built a busy page on Facebook with videos of quirky gadgets that went viral due to Joel's techniques. The videos were often stolen from rival sellers and re-cut to be internet-friendly. On

Instagram, Shopolis had 11,000 followers but on Facebook they had 305,000 likes. The last ad video they posted had 346,000 organic views and 370 comments. This is the kind of engagement that news and entertainment organisations would kill for. More attention meant more sales, and at its peak, Shopolis was generating $500,000 a month in revenue, according to Joel. There were two problems. Not only did the products hardly ever do what they claimed to, but even worse, many of Joel's customers were not receiving what they ordered. In fact they often didn't receive anything at all. The money was leaving their accounts and nothing would arrive in the post. Cheated customers would try and contact the company, but nobody would reply.

One woman calling herself Betty paid for seven 'mini-helicopter balls' as Christmas presents. None of them turned up. When she tried to contact the company, she was met with silence. Brandon was a retired policeman who reached out after his wife's order never arrived either. 'Take it from a retired police detective, who worked on a financial crimes task force, this is "theft by swindle" in its finest form. Have filed a dispute on my wife's behalf with PayPal,' he wrote on the review website Trustpilot, where Shopolis has a shocking 98 per cent poor rating. The company was accused of fraud by infuriated customers, who began reporting it to their credit card companies and the Better Business Bureau in the US. Complaints still litter the Shopolis social media page as I write this. Alice, another of the company's thousands of customers, tried to contact the company online. 'I get no answer on my support email request. I'm fucking angry. Waiting on my order since June … answer my damn emails. I paid already!' Again there was no reply. It was as if the company did not exist. Of course, in many ways it did not. Shopolis marketed goods, but as far as they saw it, they did not deliver them.

Complaints to the Better Business Bureau led to Shopolis eventually being shut down by Shopify. But Joel and Joseph just opened up a new shop under a new name. To Joel this was just an occupational hazard, and the challenge was to make as much money as possible before the game was up. 'The majority of dropshipping parts are coming from China. You're talking about two to three weeks shipping times. With Amazon, it takes around two days, sometimes same day. You can't take two weeks to ship, so you're getting all these charge-backs and then people get pissed off and they go leave bad reviews and then they report you to PayPal and then to your merchant and then Shopify. So even if you're fulfilling these orders and you're doing the best to make everyone happy, the dropshipping timeline doesn't allow for that to really succeed much longer … your store gets shut down whether that's because you lost your merchant processor or Shopify's like "you've got too many complaints" or your content is copyrighted material from another toy company … You are basically going on the internet, looking for already generated content that another company has probably spent thousands [making] and you're taking that content, finding that product cheap in China, you're plugging it into your marketing funnel, you're making a ton of money and you're shutting it down.'

Sitting in the lobby of LA's most glamorous hotel, Joel expressed no sympathy for the faceless customers who had lost money from trusting his company. In his eyes, this was the price of running a dropshipping business. He was merely trying to beat the system with the cards he had been given as an immigrant without Ivy League credentials. Despite his huge ill-gotten revenues, when Shopolis was shut down by the authorities he still found himself in debt. 'On the front end we were killing it. Our videos were getting millions of views, our CPA [cost per action] was very low, but we over-hired, overpaid, we didn't have anyone on the team that was like a financial expert so we didn't do substantial financial reporting, we had no P&L [profit and loss statement]. We kind of just made all this money and started going to dinner every night and started renting Lamborghinis and started living in fancy Beverly Hills buildings and so when you do that and you have no real idea of what your profit margin is, one day you wake up and it's like oh shit, I thought we were making all this money but really we're actually losing money.'

When Shopolis was wound down, Joel claims the company owed $300,000. To pay the debt off, he and Joseph launched yet another dropshipping site, which sold toys in the run-up to Christmas. 'The store made $2m in the month of December. This was right around when Toys 'R' Us went bankrupt and we were able to capitalise.' The newly founded JoyToys created a nightmare scenario for duped parents, who had nothing to give their children on Christmas morning. One punter called Catherine placed a gift order but received nothing. After she bombarded the JoyToys website, Joel's team sent her an email on 4 January, almost two weeks after Christmas Day. They apologised for the delay, blamed the merchant processor and promised to compensate her with a gift card. Three months later, Catherine had still received nothing. JoyToys has since been shut down too. Despite this, Joel does not think of himself as a scammer, but just another underdog trying to get a small piece of the American pie, one of many hustlers with big dreams hoping to achieve them with a smartphone and a clutch of social media accounts, going up against the might of Big Tech with the help of hacks.

'A way that ... every dropshipper has made a lot of money is by being able to pay people who have access to large celebrity networks.' What Joel meant was that dropshippers were paying kickbacks to the PR reps who had access to the social media accounts of their pop star and influencer clients so they would secretly share ads on those pages to tens of millions of followers. 'Why is Facebook so powerful? Because of the share option. Things can snowball.' He told me about a 30-second viral product video that linked to his dropshipping store and gained 50,000 comments in 48 hours.

What he was describing was manufactured shares, which Facebook had banned after being overrun by nefarious dropshippers and scammers like Joel who were drowning the site in them. Facebook and Google have a market dominance of digital adverts. The platforms make money by charging ecommerce sites to run their promotions, but Joel was using manufactured shares as a way to avoid paying, in breach of Facebook's rules. 'They've really made it a thing in the last six months where they started to send cease-and-desists to people and they announced it to the public, "manufactured sharing is not okay," but the reality is the reason Facebook is doing that is because it takes away their earned dollars, because the results that we were getting from manufactured sharing were 20 times higher than what we were getting from paying Facebook for advertising.'

Part of Joel's strategy was making his manufactured shares invisible to moderators. 'When you go on a newsfeed you can hide a post, so when I go to a feed, if you go to any celebrity page you're not gonna see it on the feed, it's hidden.' The ad would be missing from the celebrity's main feed but could still be seen by its followers on theirs.

In response, not only has Facebook launched a crack-down on rogues like Joel and changed the algorithm, but it has also attempted to increase watch time on the platform through so-called 'Watch' pages administered to specialist content makers. Remarkably, Joel claims he managed to obtain a lucrative Watch page from corrupt workers at the company: 'Their own employees were taking cash bribes like "hey I'm gonna give you $5K make sure I get this page" and they were going in the back end, enabling it for us or the community and letting you run. Facebook is a billion-dollar company who does very well and whose own employees have exploited the success of the influencers, the creators, the dropshippers. I've never *personally* paid anyone at Facebook. I've never sent money to a person at Facebook, but we've paid people who've paid people.'

Joel claims to have bootlegged four Facebook Watch pages that were eventually taken down by the tech giant. 'Shopolis had a Watch page and it was an ecommerce store. That was never supposed to happen, that was not what it was meant for.' He says he spent up to $30,000 in bribes to Facebook workers for pages that would drive sales. 'We've definitely made it back ten-fold, for sure.' Facebook's crack-down has made it harder for bootleggers like Joel. The company now has stricter policies and is more aware of the shortcuts being taken on their platform. 'They delete your Facebook, they delete your Instagram, they do a lot of stuff to like basically punish you, so you know it's adapted. [But] there's always ways. Human beings always find a way,' he says philosophically.

Joel was locked into a game against the all-powerful machines that had cornered the market of attention. 'Why should you be penalised for finding a way to market your product, right? You're not hurting anyone. You're not stealing. You're not causing damage to anyone else, you're just finding a loophole. I don't think those things should be punished, they should be celebrated.' His lamentations won't mean much to the thousands of customers who were scammed by his dropshipping sites and now found themselves out of pocket after buying cheaply mass-produced goods that never arrived.

If the promise of wealth exists anywhere on the internet, it is in the $25.6tn ecommerce industry,[5] which drives the influencer industry. As only 20 per cent of commerce happens online,[6] the influencer market is unlikely to be anywhere near its peak, especially as the barriers to entry are so low.[7] The appeal is that anyone can join the game, and as precarity grows more likely, they will. Joel's story may look unique, but it is only a matter of time before all of us are buying and selling something (most likely ourselves) online. The most successful are those hacking the big platforms and finding ways around the rules. However, the real problems arise when they find themselves in breach of the law and in the firing line of the authorities.

7

OUTSIDER TRADING

The 1980s blockbuster *Wall Street* about the fictional insider trader Gordon Gekko was supposed to be a moral warning on corporate greed yet by accident became one of Wall Street's most successful recruitment videos. Thirty years later and the penny-stock fraudster Jordan Belfort, now immortalised by Leonardo DiCaprio in the film *The Wolf of Wall Street*, has done the same thing for the social media generation. Today, pictures of DiCaprio's Belfort have been turned into motivational quotes and hustle inspiration for a generation so hyper-consumerist it would make the hedonistic 1980s blush.

Now approaching 60 years old, the real Jordan Belfort has a million Instagram followers despite his fraud conviction. He is idolised online by a generation that has turned his life story into an escape route from rags to riches. He makes a lucrative income on the get-rich-quick speakers' circuit. Facebook happily promotes his posts; adoring young men choose to follow him online; and his seminars sell out. Nobody cares that he defrauded ordinary working men and women when being ordinary is itself a crime. Social media platforms incentivise you to invent who you want to be, and there is nothing worse than failing to fight your way to the top, even if you have to scam your way to get there.

Belfort's protégés, these same adoring young men, are now themselves accruing huge followings pretending to be millionaire currency traders. In reality they are aggressively signing up vulnerable young adults, teenagers and even children to an international pyramid scheme that has helped to generate billions for unregulated companies selling risky financial trading products. They are the wolves of Instagram, social media influencers dressed in financial analyst clothing.

Wolves of Instagram

In 2017, I interviewed a young man named Elijah Oyefeso for the *Guardian* newspaper. The then 21-year-old south Londoner had been fast gaining attention with his own rags-to-riches tale. Elijah was a university drop-out from a poor neighbourhood who was now making a killing as a self-made financial whiz-kid. He would broadcast his trades from his mansion in the woods, post videos of himself driving an electric-blue Rolls-Royce with a silver bonnet while wearing a bathrobe, and encourage young people to apply for opportunities with his trading company, Dreams Come True Ltd. He claimed that thousands did, especially once he really hit the big time.

In his old neighbourhood, Elijah was celebrated like a local hero. To impressionable teenagers he was an inspiration. After gaining hundreds of thousands of followers online, he even caught the attention of the mainstream press, and his exploits went viral. His story was reported by leading British newspapers like the *Daily Mail*, *The Sun* and *The Times*. He was even profiled in the Channel 4 documentary series *Rich Kids Go Shopping*. According to a close friend, once Elijah was broadcast to the nation, his fame blew up and he was inundated with requests from around the country to join his trading floor. But there was a problem. Elijah's company did not have a trading floor. It did not even have an office.

Dreams Come True was not registered at Companies House. It didn't exist as anything more than a website and some social media accounts. Elijah had posted videos from a mansion he claimed was his, but on paper he actually lived in his family home on a south-east London council estate. His entire life was a fantasy.

The deception was finally revealed when Elijah appeared at Southampton Crown Court on charges of dangerous driving and possession of a weapon. The self-styled trader was found guilty of ploughing his car into a friend to whom he owed money, a claim he contested. During the trial the judge remarked: '[You] portrayed yourself as a very successful trader within the financial market. Clearly this is not the case.' Elijah's own lawyer even told the court that his client 'makes a number of claims about his wealth but I have seen no evidence of this … Clearly if he had this money he could have written a cheque to the victim.'[1] Elijah was exposed as a fraud by his own counsel.

Elijah told me he considered himself to be an 'influencer', and had even attempted to launch an agency hawking his online fame to the highest bidder. The way he had really made money was in covertly working on behalf of rogue trading platforms selling risky financial instruments that in some cases were revealed to be entirely rigged. These products included the volatile 'contracts for difference' and the now-banned binary options, which are considered no-win betting products. The companies he worked for ranged from the legitimate but predatory to the outright fraudulent. The stocky university drop-out would lure in teenagers and young adults with limited knowledge of the money markets by posting images of luxury goods he claimed to have bought with his winnings. At the time, one teenager told me that he and his friends were drawn in by the sight of a young black man succeeding in the old white man's world of finance. Once someone got in touch with Elijah online, he or an unpaid minion would message: 'I'm offering a great opportunity to earn £100–400+ per week from trading, no experience required, all done from home and only requires 15–30 min per day.'

What he was failing to declare was that each of the trading platforms his young victims signed up to (with a minimum deposit of £250) paid him around £40–80 – and that it was the recruitment process itself, rather than betting on these predatory financial products, that made him his money. In other words, he was an affiliate marketer, and he told me he had managed to recruit thousands of investors. It is almost impossible to count the number of marketing affiliates masquerading as successful traders on Instagram, but we can count the number of promotional posts they've made using hashtags such as #BinaryOptions (5.9 million), #TraderLifestyle (1.4 million) and #RichKidsOfInstagram (1.5 million).[2] Those numbers rise by the minute, and the thousands of accounts generating them appear and disappear constantly.

In a challenging jobs market, affiliate work often appears the most accessible route to money to those under pressure. There is no interview or licence required, and pay is by commission only. All that is needed, in most cases, is an email address and a bank account. As marketers do not earn a set wage or salary, they provide a growing class of cheap labour to exploitative industries like fast fashion and betting. The most scandalous of Elijah's paymasters was Banc de Binary, which, like many of these new financial platforms, was founded in Israel after the 2008 financial crash. Israeli firms have the advantage of having access to European markets without being burdened by European regulators, which makes them even more prone to bad behaviour.

The man at the helm of Banc de Binary was Oren Shabat Laurent, a former Israeli paratrooper. At its peak, the company had a yearly revenue of $100m. It sought respectability by sponsoring football teams such as Liverpool and Southampton, but both clubs dropped it once it became embroiled in scandal. It faced a string of multimillion-dollar lawsuits from clients, and was pursued by the U.S. Securities and Exchange Commission, which fined it $11m for major regulatory breaches such as using shell offices in the UK and the US to evade financial regulations. It was kicked out of the US in 2013. Soon after that, it was denied access to European markets when it lost its licence in Israel. In January 2017, the company ceased trading when it was revealed to have used software rigged against its users. This provoked sheer indifference from Elijah. Not only was he happy to affiliate for the company; he was openly breaking the law encouraging children under 18 to sign up and bet.

In the past, it would have taken a skilful and charismatic confidence artist to convince so many people of the success Elijah had claimed, but the 21-year-old was neither smart nor charming. His knowledge of finance and economics was limited and he was barely able to express the little he knew coherently. He has a high-pitched voice, slurs his words and stutters, but with a smartphone and social media apps even he could wear a convincing disguise. Elijah is just one of a pack of hundreds of thousands of young internet influencers now dabbling in deception.

Today, Britain's Financial Conduct Authority (FCA) is drowning in complaints that come in faster than they can take action. Many of the victims are impressionable kids taken in by influencers like Elijah. The FCA found that youngsters under 25 were six times more likely to trust an investment offer received through social media,[3] a world defined by manufactured realities. In 2020, Action Fraud, the UK's national reporting centre for fraud and cyber crime, saw the number of complaints triple within three years.[4]

One of the most successful influencers I have come across marketing trading as a way to earn extra cash was twenty-something Samuel Leach, who styled himself as a working-class boy made good. However, despite his perfect Instagram feed, I managed to speak to a string of people who regretted ever meeting him. David first came across Leach whilst trying to find work. In 2014, David was newly wed with a heavily pregnant wife. 'I had my own building company,' the 36-year-old told me proudly over the phone, but 'I suffered a spinal injury so we had to find some sort of money fast. I couldn't go to work.' He began a frantic search through listings on job sites before coming across a vacancy for a junior trader with the carefully styled Samuel & Co. Trading. The company described itself as 'a fund in London, with client accounts across the globe'. David did not fit the profile for an entry-level corporate job. He had a receding hairline, was in his mid thirties and was a construction worker by trade. Nevertheless, the generous salary range of £25,000–110,000 per annum caught his attention. 'My sister works in London,' he said. 'She said with trading if it works for you, you can potentially be very comfortable.' So he fired off an application. 'You know the chips are all down, [so I thought] let's try it basically and potentially you got to be in it [to win it].'

David was not the only one to be enticed by the vacancy. Luke was just 21 when he applied. 'I'd recently been made redundant. I was fortunate enough to get quite a nice payout. I'd always had a fascination regarding financial markets and trading and I guess who doesn't at a young age. I'm sure everyone's seen *Wolf of Wall Street*, it's one of the things I guess you aspire to.' That allure had already influenced 29-year-old Michael. He had just started dabbling in the markets and was looking for work in finance when he too found the vacancy at Samuel & Co. He emailed his CV in.

What none of these men knew was that there was never any contract of employment on offer. All three were inadvertently applying for an expensive fraternity consisting of opulent parties orchestrated for social media. It was all the fiefdom of a digital Jay Gatsby – Samuel Leach.

I interviewed Samuel, a self-described influencer, in 2018 for a newspaper article I never filed. By then, he and his company Samuel Leach & Co. Ltd had amassed over 600,000 followers across social media, including 132,000 YouTube subscribers and over 470,000 on Instagram. His social media accounts were peppered with photos of sports cars and holidays in rented super-homes, *Wolf of Wall Street* memes and financial explainer videos. Samuel has been regularly profiled by the aspirational hustle page Rich Kids of Instagram. In reality this page, with 800,000 followers at the time, generated revenue by charging brands and individuals who wanted to gain more followers £60 for a featured post, although without informing their young acolytes that those profiled were self-promoters. Samuel also hired a swanky PR agent and became a regular contributor to the *Sunday Express*, where he is presented as a 'Bitcoin millionaire'. Ahead of our meeting, his 'executive assistant', Kathy, was keen to let me know how busy he was. 'Please advise if you would like this slot as soon as possible before it gets booked up,' she said. I took it.

Although the company described itself as a London fund, it was actually based in Watford, where its young founder lived. When I arrived at the shared offices it leased, Samuel was in a buoyant mood and regaled me with his success since founding the business in 2012. 'The team has grown exponentially from one person to nearly 67 traders, so there is a large amount of us in the UK, Europe and it just carried on growing.'

Leach is around five foot nine and stocky. His Instagram captures his gym progress, along with what he calls his trader 'journey', which found him micro-fame in the digital community of young financial enthusiasts. He is prolific on YouTube and his channel has amassed over 21 million views. He once posted his video call with a burly believer from the US who was in tears of joy at speaking to such an illustrious trader. 'I have fans and people who will come and ask for a photo,' Samuel told me. 'One of our fans sent us a hoodie to sign and send off to him, it's nice to see it. I get a lot of stuff like that,' he humbly boasted, before telling me his origin story. It's a tale I've heard before and a big part of Samuel's pitch. 'I came from a broken background,' he says. Whilst studying marketing and advertising at the University of Hertfordshire, he secured an internship at the prestigious private bank C. Hoare & Co., though it never materialised into a career. Instead, Samuel used his student loan to trade stocks, later telling the *Watford Observer* that he turned £2,000 into £178,000 over the course of a year. He set up Samuel & Co. Trading in 2012.

On social media, Samuel & Co. Trading has described and marketed itself as a hedge fund, an investment vehicle for high-net-worth and institutional investors, who usually have funds starting in the millions. However, according to past Companies House reports, the company registered profits of £33,978 in 2017, up from £1,285 in 2016, when Samuel first began framing it as a major player in finance.[5] He settled on calling it a 'prop fund' and claimed to invest anywhere between £2,000 and £50,000 in his so-called junior traders.

When David learnt that he had been shortlisted to be one of Samuel's traders, following a robust telephone interview, he was nervous. 'I thought I was going to throw up, to be honest. I've always been self-employed [and] it was the first job interview I ever had.' He confirmed his attendance at the second interview and profusely thanked the company in a message.

On his arrival at the interview, he was encouraged by members of the company to sell himself, and advanced into a training programme with the dozen other hopefuls in a low-grade St Albans hotel. He recalls a trend among them. 'So, yeah, I'm sitting here, I'm not a snob by any means but I'm thinking how the hell did all these guys qualify. There was quite a few builders. Then there's a few others who basically looked like they were fresh out of school and had no dealings of the world whatsoever and to me this was meant to be quite a prestigious thing. [That's] the way it was sold.'

Luke and Michael both described the same process and outcome. Both qualified for the introductory course, which cost £1,200 and was run by the company's senior traders, who were in their twenties. 'They're basically salesmen, none of them trade,' said Luke. 'It's packaged as a two-week thing but really you're in the office for two or three days. They pass everyone. Why wouldn't they? Everyone's a big bag of cash. To them you are a customer not a future employee. So their whole idea is to bullshit you into believing you are going into a role. During the course, they promise you and promise you that there's a job in it, that you're going to come in full time and be paid full time, that kind of thing, when really there is not.'

Leach admitted to me in 2018 that at the time, the company only had one full-time employee: him. But despite the revelation that the job they had applied for was actually a course in disguise, David, Luke and Michael all agreed to pay the fees. 'I kind of went with it. At the time

I was trying to grab hold of anything. I was flat broke if I'm being honest with you. It took the last of my savings to pay for the course,' said David. All three men describe the actual programme as informative, with unusual but effective features. 'You do a bit of mindset training with Adrian Leach, who happens to be Samuel's dad! He does a bit of hypnotherapy on you. It's a very strange session,' said Luke, but David described it as 'bang on', and both admit that overall they enjoyed it. The company then set up demo accounts for their recruits to trade on, with the promise of a substantial financial investment in anyone who could make it rain.

'He made out that the investment was a largish invest-ment and basically from him personally, and that you'd have a share of 50:50 of the profits,' David said. 'Now I had a hell of a week and I did not meet that criteria, but the guys who did, the investment was like £200!' A fraction of the £2,000 minimum investment Leach had outlined to me. 'We had a thing called "1 per cent risk in a trade" so potentially they would have made £10 to £20 in a week even if they traded on point [successfully], which is impossible to make a living on. From what I've been told from some of the guys who are [still] there, they weren't even covering their travel into the office.' All three applicants claimed they did not receive any investment from Samuel, but their failure to secure either a job or investment did not end their association. They continued trading under his tutelage with their own savings through brokers that Samuel had a commercial relationship with.

Michael claims that he had saved a decent amount from a plumbing job he had had since he was 16 years old, and used some of it to rent a desk from Samuel for £600 a month, despite losing thousands on bad trades while working there. If the losses were vexing, the community gave him solace. In addition to posting selfie videos taken on million-pound yachts off the coast of Turkey with captions like 'Millionaire Trader Lifestyle', Samuel has an appetite for hosting parties and BBQs at his place for his recruits of mostly millennial men. 'This is what we call the Samuel & Co. family,' he says in a video posted to YouTube. In another he appears to take the 'family' to a $10m mansion where they swig champagne, play pranks on one another and live in luxury.

However, if the getaways looked like a company perk, the truth was less glamorous. 'They were good, but you needed to pay for yourself. Everyone was paying to go,' said Michael. '[We'd] trade. Drink. Party. It was a good laugh at times.' Samuel's posts of holidays and parties paint him as a modern Jay Gatsby, but whereas F. Scott Fitzgerald's protagonist threw parties for the attention of a single woman, Leach throws his for a community of ambitious young men desperate to be part of his success.

Michael claimed to have lost £12,000 whilst being initiated into the gang.

'I was there over a year. I weren't getting paid. I was assisting in helping students once I got profitable. People would inbox me directly and I would direct them to Samuel himself. Marketing on Instagram.' Samuel has a skill for befriending young men and demanding loyalty. 'The lads he had in the office were running his training programme for him. You know, he was not physically doing it himself, which was smart on his part because he was basically earning money without lifting a finger.' As time went on, Michael lost a further £16,000, induced by Samuel's new automated trading algorithm 'Fusion', which he aggressively marketed via the company's Instagram. He hawked the automated programme for £3,000, with a finance (loan) option, and claimed it had an 80 per cent win ratio. 'It's his programme but it's linked with a broker from the algorithm that he makes commission from,' Michael told me. He said that when he worked there, the broker was AxiTrader, an Australian company that specialised in the controversial contract for difference (CFD) products, where you bet on whether a price will rise or fall without actually owning it. The product has been heavily scrutinised by the UK's Financial Conduct Authority.

'They [the 'employees'] are all trading their own funds,' believes David. 'You pay your blind to enter the game. They call that your spread. Sam would make money on those spreads off those lads. They're using his trading platform. Sam would agree with those [brokerage] companies to use them but would get a royalty and would push these platforms along to people and make money on them, so he's getting them again.' Former traders also allege that Samuel was charging everyone trading through him a one-off fee of £200 and then a further charge of £200 to be paid monthly. In other words, they were not employees but subscribers who were sold a well-packaged dream: a model I've seen over and over again from this type of influencer CEO.

'I made nothing trading,' said David. 'A friend tried to invest in me just to help me out and get me going. I lost him a grand and a half. Of my own money I lost £700 and with funds being so tight I said this isn't for me. I just said "forget it, be a big boy and go and get a proper job", All three men have quit trading, but Samuel has found an abundance of new customers from a never-ending conveyor belt of enthusiasts from social media.

The crypto craze

The much-maligned CFDs that were Samuel's bread and butter have lost popularity online to Bitcoin. The decentralised cryptocurrency created in the aftermath of the banking crisis by an anonymous computer programmer was worth $0.003 when the first exchange opened for it in March 2010. Eleven years later, Bitcoin was selling for an astonishing $61,283.80. If you had invested just $10 in Bitcoin, you could have cashed out with $204,279,333.33. Investing $200 would have made you a billionaire.

The currency has become pegged to the hype of novice speculators mobilised by influencer investors. The coin is the definition of volatile and will to rise to extraordinary heights and crash to staggering lows. Bitcoin hit $1 in 2011 then crashed. Hit $266 in 2013 then crashed. Hit $1,000 in 2014 then crashed again. In 2020, after tweets by Elon Musk, the billionaire with a cult following, the coin quadrupled in value.[6] Each boom and bust has brought in a new wave of speculators and fans gripped by a currency most people in the world still don't understand – including its investors. Bitcoin is enabled by a technology called blockchain, which everyone seems to explain differently. The general idea is that it is a decentralised record of transactions that is stored across different computers, almost like a shared Google doc but without the all-powerful central authority. Everyone with a code or key can access it, and the software issues new codes and records them based on the commands of the old ones.

If you are confused, it is because blockchain is confusing, but what is easier to understand is that the currency can be traded anonymously without being easily traced. The belief that its anonymity makes it valuable is what drives consumer faith in it, despite it being impractical as a daily currency, unprotected by governments, too volatile to be used for saving and having no universally accepted intrinsic value like gold. It is this herd behaviour that started the newest and biggest gold rush, featuring crypto geeks, gamblers and ordinary working people with fears of missing out. In 2017 and 2020, news of Bitcoin's rise was everywhere. It was on the front of tabloids and the gossip in launderettes, but the arena it dominated most was that of social media. Overnight, more and more new platforms claiming to be portals to exchange fiat money like pounds and dollars into cryptocurrency were pushing Bitcoin. Many of the influencers were promoting such sites to their followers but were not declaring that they were, of course, doing so for commission from sign-ups.

The early adopters, as usual, were the real winners, but that did not stop those late to the party from trying to gatecrash the spoils. There were reports of ordinary investors remortgaging their homes and taking out bank loans to get a slice of Bitcoin, further fuelling the bubble. In 2017, a friend of mine put a sizeable chunk of his life savings into the cryptocurrency a week or two before the price peaked, in the hope of turning a quick profit. At one point his beginner's luck was going so well he even suggested packing in his job to become a fund manager. Then Bitcoin started skydiving, until by 2018 it had lost up to 80 per cent of its value. The price had been massively inflated by both the fear of missing out and foul play. Yet by 2021 it was more than three times its 2017 peak. Sadly, my friend had already cashed out.

In the run-up to the 2017 boom and bust, up to 40 per cent of all Bitcoins were estimated to be in the hands of just 1,000 people.[7] The size of these whales in a sea of investors meant that the news that one of them was to sell a fraction of their holdings could single-handedly collapse the price. Equally, a move to buy could send the value rocketing. Historically, manipulating positive news to increase the demand for a stock has been a way to drive up the price before selling it at an inflated figure. The illegal tactic, better known as 'pump and dump', is prohibited because markets need our trust to function. Yet soon the crypto surge appeared to be the result of just such a ploy.

Writing in *Vox*, William Harris, the former CEO of PayPal, called Bitcoin 'a colossal pump and dump scheme, the likes of which the world has never seen' in an article headlined 'Bitcoin is the greatest scam in history'.[8] A research paper by finance professors John Griffin and Amin Shams at the University of Texas and Ohio State University suggested that Bitcoin's surge towards $20,000 was the result of market manipulation by a single investor.

Even the U.S. Securities and Exchange Commission expressed concern about rising Bitcoin fraud, considering how frequently it is misrepresented by those with hidden commercial interests.[9] All money is imagined, but at least the currencies printed by governments have some power behind them, and some use. However, Bitcoin, with zero use to the average person, somehow rose to be 67,000 times more valuable than the dollar in 2021.

During Bitcoin's booms, the huge appetite for the next valuable cryptocurrency started a wave of new coin offerings launched by chancers with exaggerated claims. The technology behind Bitcoin was a genuine innovation, but many of the coins now being boosted online by influencers are cheap imitations deploying pump and dump techniques. In 2018, a concerned US Commodity Futures Trading Commission warned that 'fraud is now occurring using little known virtual currencies and digital coins or tokens, but thanks to mobile messaging apps or Internet message boards, today's pump-and dumpers don't need a physical boiler room [like the *Wolf of Wall Street*], they organize anonymously and hype the currencies and tokens using social media. Some of these pump-and-dump groups and chat rooms contain thousands of members. The members subscribe to the group and follow the conversations as they indicate when the next pump-and-dump will occur.'[10]

Coin offerings are where influencer and start-up culture appear one and the same. A culture where nothing needs to be intrinsically valuable or true about a commodity, where all that matters is being able to influence enough people so that hype is generated and that is where the value comes from. Cryptocurrencies have become a marketer's dream, and operators like Samuel Leach can find hordes of willing victims all over social media. The Bitcoin price rise in 2017 initially brought Samuel to the mines equipped with a fleet of newly purchased high-powered Antminer D3 computers, each costing about £2,000. 'We had like eight or ten D3s and got them set up in there. It just sounds like a Harrier jet,' he laughed. 'It's crazy and the amount of heat that they give off, even with the air conditioning set, it's like sitting in a sauna.'

Samuel posted a YouTube video in 2017 for his followers flaunting his setup, titled 'Printing Money'. But, as time went on, his takings were relatively modest and when I spoke to him, he estimated that each machine made an average of £5 a day. Considering the volatility of crypto, influencers have found that an easier way to profit from the crypto craze is to create a new coin. After seeing a series of silly coins flooding social media, Samuel thought there was potential. So, he decided to join the party.

Yield Coin was one of the hundreds of new cryptocurrencies launched within the space of months in 2018. Most new currencies are worthless; they are primarily a way to generate money using unregulated virtual tokens, each with a carefully curated identity to capture buyers. For lines of code that have no intrinsic worth, their value lies in the buzz that can be generated – and few know how to stoke hype better than Samuel. His open Telegram group contained more than 1,500 members, and all became engaged with his coin. 'It's just mental to see the kind of reach that this kind of stuff can get and the community. We're like what do you guys want and they're like merchandise! This is a crypto, this isn't a clothing line, but if that's what you want …'

The UK's FCA has raised concerns over the potential for fraud given the downgraded protections afforded to investors. New cryptocurrencies are sold through digital brochures called white papers, mission statements that can be unbalanced or misleading. Samuel's paper promised that his 'collective community of 1,800 traders worldwide are ready to adopt'[11] Yield Coin, and that Samuel & Co. would remunerate its high-performing employees in the currency. However, he failed to mention that he was the company's sole full-time member of staff and that the bulk of its traders were novices learning on his courses. Even the 'executive assistant' who curtly emailed me turned out to be his mother.

At the time of writing, Samuel's coin is worth $0.001, having fallen 97 per cent since its all-time high in 2018, according to CoinGecko, an aggregator of crypto data. Despite this, his company has flourished from the success of selling courses to novices, earning a cut from introducing them to brokers and ad revenue from YouTube. In 2019, it posted cash reserves of over £2m,[12] likely boosted by his coin. Samuel claimed he was trying to sign up more companies to back Yield Coin, but underpinning his plan for the expansion of the currency was his own company, whose most consistent source of income since incorporation had come from recruiting applicants with a ruse that their training fees were a prelude to a full-time job.

In the corner of the internet where Samuel is famous, his bravado is a currency of its own. In these digital communities, young men and older men desperate to regain control of their lives talk all night on messenger apps about the commodities they think will help them do just that. Surfing the money markets appears a lucrative sport at a time when people are being told that their worth is tied to their wealth. It is online where the new digital bucket shops and boiler rooms breathe. A generation of young self-styled gurus are building micro-fame out of manufactured lives. First they fake it and then they make it. Although plenty have personally paid the price, Samuel Leach now actually has a multimillion-pound business, and he's not the only one.

'Your network is my net worth'

In early 2020, just before the COVID crisis really hit, the sister of one of my old school friends posted on Instagram that she wanted to help her followers make more money. She was putting an evening together at an east London college for those frustrated with their jobs, using the caption 'Teaching you the secrets of the banks'. I decided to sign up. When I arrived, the room was noticeably mixed race and inter-generational, but of the 30 people present, most were young adults aged between 18 and 24. There were young men in streetwear sitting alongside greying women edging towards retirement age. I took a seat next to three giggling teenagers.

At the front of the lecture room, a twenty-something brunette with an old-school East End accent promised that we were about to be offered a 'life-changing skill'. Briony told the room that she had graduated from university several years earlier but had found it hard to gain steady employment and had found herself on a downward spiral, falling into debt and depression. All that changed when she joined the Amey Finance Academy, the company hosting tonight's seminar. The lecture had the feel of an evangelical church convention where members of the congregation declare how Jesus changed their life right before a collection is made. It was not long before I learnt who Briony's saviour was.

Des Amey, the apparent founder of the company, was the final speaker of the night. He strutted onstage wearing a flat cap, a double-breasted navy jacket and a burgundy turtleneck. 'Everything changes now!' he exclaimed. What Des claimed to be offering was the chance to join his company as a financial trader. He promised that Amey Finance could teach you how to make a good living buying and selling foreign currencies like the US dollar or Japanese yen. Anybody can learn and have a chance to make life-changing money, he said, adding that he was not only earning a 'six-figure income' but was helping the working class create 'generational wealth'. He boasted that he had acquired a trading floor in Canary Wharf with up to 20 traders – but as with Samuel, none of them were on the payroll.

Amey Finance had no employees. You paid the company to join it. Despite being UK-registered, it was just one face of an American company ringing alarm bells across Europe, a franchise of the giant multi-level marketing company International Markets Live (IML), which had obtained a foothold in the UK thanks to salesmen like Des targeting the desperation of new graduates, young mothers and those facing a life on low incomes. Social media was once again instrumental.

Des carefully cultivated his Instagram with splashes of glamour and motivation. Most interesting was how his following would spike to almost 20,000 followers, then drop by 75 per cent, a result of using bot accounts to make him look more popular than he actually was. The product he was selling was another type of contract for difference, the financial instrument where you bet on whether a price will rise or fall without actually owning the currency. Not only are betting products like these volatile, but according to an investigation by Britain's Financial Conduct Authority, 82 per cent of all trades are lost, with the average punter losing over £2,200 a year. Politicians have even called financial instruments like this 'no-win gambling products'. Despite the authorities cracking down on the way they are sold, products like this have formed the backbone of an aggressive marketing industry, with companies like Amey Finance and International Markets Live claiming they can help you master the markets if you pay a significant subscription fee for their services. Trading with IML will cost a novice over £1,200 a year in fees, but they're likely to lose even more.

The FCA have issued warnings not just about the kind of products International Markets Live sells but about the company itself, with a note on 'how to protect yourself from scammers'. In 2018, they warned UK consumers against the company, stating: 'This firm is not authorised by us and is targeting people in the UK. Based upon information we hold, we believe it is carrying on regulated activities which require authorisation.'[13] The company's response to growing criticism was to change their brand name to the IM Mastery Academy. In 2018, they had a membership of over 110,000, but just two years later their most senior marketers claimed they had grown to 500,000 globally[14] and were approaching revenue of $1bn after an exponential increase driven by high-profile influencers with millions of followers and affiliate micro-influencers like Des. In a familiar story, Des presented himself as a successful financial trader, yet earned the bulk of his money in recruiting. Briony, his number two, spun this side of the company as their 'leadership programme' and a way to 'help others to achieve their dreams'. 'You do get paid handsomely,' she told the room.

The day after Briony's presentation, I sat down with Des in a private restaurant at One Canada Square, in Canary Wharf. He told me his own route into IM had been conventional. He was born in 1980, which just about makes him a millennial. He and his family moved to the industrial town of Dagenham from his native Ghana when he was a toddler. Today, he is as East End as pie and mash. In the early 1980s, Dagenham, on the borders of east London and Essex, was a white working-class community built around what was then Europe's biggest car assembly plant. At its peak, Ford's Dagenham factory employed 40,000 people. When Des's family arrived, he recalls that they were one of maybe three black families in the town. 'We adjusted pretty well, we were accepted,' he says. When he was seven or eight years old, his father left. 'Money was scarce but at the same time we weren't poor. We got by scrimping and saving. No family holidays, just the bare basics.'

He describes his former secondary school, Robert Clack, as one of the worst in the country, but he managed to escape with decent GCSEs, A levels and aspirations to study at university. 'Dagenham itself is not very aspirational … most people aspired to grow up and work at Ford.' Over the years, the factory wound down, before the forces of globalisation led to the closure of the car assembly line in 2002, costing thousands of jobs. The area was facing an existential crisis due to rapid deindustrialisation and government apathy. At the same time, Prime Minister Tony Blair was adamant that the future was in the information economy, and so Des chose to study what he described as the logical choice: IT and business. 'You have to remember this was the late nineties, early 2000s. Everyone was talking about IT. It was supposed to be the next big thing.' He enrolled at the University of East London. The former polytechnic was shaping up for the new millennium with a huge investment in a new campus on the old Royal Docks, hoping to leverage its proximity to the City of London and Canary Wharf.

Despite obtaining a degree during the boom in information technology services, Des failed to secure a lucrative gig after graduation. 'It just didn't really work out for me. I ended up taking a part-time job with EE – T-Mobile as it was known then. They made me store manager as soon as I graduated, and then they made me redundant.' He had hoped his time in store could launch a more senior career at the company. 'Mobile phones were just taking off and they had this brand-new shiny office in Hatfield so my plan was to kind of do that. Make a name for myself and move into the corporate side of things and become a corporate …' He tails off. 'Growing up, I always had this vision of me being a businessman, holding a briefcase, I didn't know what I was doing but that's kind of how I visualised myself, doing something like that.'

He recalls applying for corporate jobs at the company but getting nowhere. In an industry that recruited in its own image, he didn't fit in. 'I just didn't have the experience, I was just getting bounced. I applied for a couple and I wasn't even getting to interview stage and I knew why. It just didn't work out for me.'

What did work out was the staple middle-class career of teaching. Des saw an ad and applied. He entered the profession during a great push to diversify the sector and so found himself fast-tracked for managerial teaching roles. Within five years he had made it to assistant head. In this time he had got married, bought a house, started a family and was earning a good income. 'I remember turning around to my wife at the time and saying I think we've made it.' He was living a life of middle-class respectability in Britain's consumer society. However, with the holidays, the new car and the mortgage, he soon found himself in debt trying to keep up. He needed more money.

Des's school was in the shadow of Canary Wharf. It may have been just seven minutes from One Canada Square, but it was a world away from everything the skyscraper personified and everything Des found himself wanting to be part of. The allure of wealth is even more seductive when you see it daily. The moment his life really changed was when he read the financial self-help book *Rich Dad Poor Dad*. When I first saw Des in action, he even told his congregation to read Robert Kiyosaki's best seller. The book's dubious tactics were best summarised by finance reporter Helaine Olen in *Forbes* magazine: 'The tips ran the gamut from ridiculous to illegal and downright hurtful and included advocating for insider trading, arguing for the purchase of multiple real estate properties with little or no money down and telling followers they could purchase stocks on margin via unfunded brokerage accounts.'[15] It was this kind of highly leveraged investment strategy that led to the 2008 global financial crash. According to research by the US National Bureau of Economic Research[16] and the Federal Reserve Board, a rise in property investors with multiple leveraged mortgages drove the increase in mortgage defaults.[17] In 2008, over three million homes in the US entered foreclosure[18] after their owners had tried to pursue the kind of advice Kiyosaki had given, with greedy banks happy to oblige them.

In Britain, home ownership has been a national obsession since Margaret Thatcher sold off Britain's publicly owned homes. The radical policy created the largest transfer of wealth in British history[19] and made property a shrewd investment for anyone hoping to make a buck, so Des paid to go on a course to train as a mortgage broker. During the day he would teach classes and in the evening he used a franchise that enabled him to find mortgages for house buyers and loans for small businesses within his network who needed credit. He would earn commission from the loan companies for everybody he signed up, and although he claims to have made good money, he did not consider it enough.

'I was searching for something that would give me that lifestyle but also give me [free] time and that's when I fell into trading,' he tells me. 'But what really did it for me was when I fell into network marketing – that opened my eyes to entrepreneurship in a whole different light. I was able to carve out a six-figure income from network marketing in a very short space of time.'

He claims that within three months he was earning £2,000 a month from signing people up to distribute and sell International Markets Live's subscription service for novice traders under the banner of Amey Finance. 'Every time somebody signs up, they're paying £130 a month [and] that all goes to the parent company and then they pay us every Friday.' As he grew his 'team', the money started to rocket. 'Say you join and you sign up 100 people, that's 100 people for you, that's 100 people for me. The benchmark for making six figures is having 500 people in your team ... I don't know 95 per cent of the people in my team because it organically snowballs. As I'm talking to you right now, somebody's out there signing somebody right now that's going to my figures.'

Everybody joins with the hope of being able to make money, but all models of this nature will burn out as there are only so many people who can sign up. The system benefits those at the top who get in early, which is why pyramid schemes are illegal, and only the ruse of a product keeps them compliant with the law. Des is clear on what that product is: 'We've rebranded ourselves as wealth creation experts. We teach you how to create wealth, how to create generational wealth.' But the overwhelming majority make very little.

According to a leaked income disclosure statement by the company, 87 per cent of its business marketers were not making more than $52 a year, a common trend with most multi-level marketing companies and pyramid schemes.[20] Although IML at least had the cover of having customers who were not marketers, their customers had still subscribed to the company under the false promise that everyone could make more money than they lost trading FOREX. I spoke to many young mothers who had been trading with the company for over a year but had found themselves consistently losing against big finance algorithms. At times they could be up, but it would not be long before they were down again. They had become immersed in the positivity of the IML community, and blamed themselves for not applying themselves well enough. Des was also a convincing leader. His former role as an assistant head teacher gave him a sense of trustworthiness and authority. He even began to recruit former students and staff – for example, he had met Briony at school. He was relatable, and most importantly he had an extensive network of young adults who were disadvantaged but ambitious and who worshipped him like a deity.

IML does not just make its money flogging trading courses and signing up marketing recruits; it also squeezes every possible penny out of those plugged into its global community. It sells dinners, dropshipping software, and conferences where the company's top marketers are treated like prophets. The richer you appear, the more beloved you become. At ticketed business events that look more like evangelical church conventions or pop concerts, the company's biggest influencers extol the value of staying focused, to dissuade anyone from cancelling their subscription. When members register for one event, they get a call about another. A young woman told me she bought a $155 VIP ticket to IML's big winter conference and was instantly called to sign up to a £7,000 'mindset' course with a motivational speaker named Bob Proctor – a famous figure on the lucrative get-rich-quick speaker circuit, with over a million Instagram followers. Many of IML's biggest social media stars are veterans of other multi-level marketing companies and pyramid schemes and have their own core following. The biggest might be Bob Proctor's mentee, a millennial named Alex Morton.

Alex Morton's Instagram page is a trough of motivational quotes, hustle porn and slickly edited music videos curating his jet-set life. One moment he is in Trinidad, the next he is on a private flight to Latin America spreading the good news that 'you can be rich if you believe in it'. His motivational video clips are widely shared and draw heavily on the pseudoscience theology of nineteenth- and twentieth-century huckster books like the 1937 best seller *Think and Grow Rich*, which has sold over 100 million copies and has found a new audience thanks to the viral new prophets. It is a spiritual predecessor to books like

Rich Dad Poor Dad and Morton's own *Dorm Room to Millionaire: How to Dream Big, Believe Big & Achieve Big*. All preach that you attract the things you need if you just know what you want.

Alex Morton first rose to fame spearheading a controversial multi-level marketing company as a student at Arizona State University. Vemma was a self-described nutrition company that targeted indebted college students with the offer to make money working as independent distributors of its drinks products. The company was founded by a veteran entrepreneur named Benson Boreyko, who had started out working in America's biggest MLM, Amway. Although Boreyko was the CEO, once Alex joined, the then 21-year-old became the company's most recognisable face, leading a slickly manufactured campaign called the Young People Revolution that aimed to make selling the company's products appear sexy to students. It showed ordinary college freshmen living a fraternity boy's dream in private jets and designer clothes by selling Vemma's drinks and products.[21]

Vemma presented its model as an alternative way to cover the mounting debts of college tuition, and told students that for an initial investment of $600 and a mandatory minimum of $150 in product purchases per month, they could earn between $500 and $50,000 a month.[22] In reality, 97 per cent would have made more money in a job paying the minimum wage, and 40 per cent made less than $79 a month, which didn't even cover the monthly subscription. Morton's response to criticism was that very few people made it to the top in any field in capitalism, so how was their pyramid structure any different to the way of the world? He had a point.

Despite near-certain odds of failure, thousands continued to put money into Vemma's coffers, enticed by the image Alex curated. Students facing mounting debts were now even further out of pocket and under financial pressure. In 2016, the Federal Trade Commission shut the company down, calling it a 'pyramid scheme'.[23] Vemma and CEO Boreyko were banned from using the business model and given minor fines that paled in comparison to the company's $200m revenues.[24] As for Alex, rather than being shamed into anonymity, the millennial had now demonstrated to every MLM huckster in the country that he had a gift for the ruthless sale. He was in demand. Today, he and his mentor Proctor are treated like messiahs in the IML community, where they are high-ranking speakers and affiliates. According to Alex, his huge influence is single-handedly responsible for signing up 90,000 people to IML.[25]

On his website, Alex claims that his work is now dedicated to giving back. 'I have seen good people struggle for so long, and I want to help. Yes, I've earned over

$10,000,000, but it's not about the money. It's about giving people the power to take back their own lives.' If this sounds as though he is embarking on a charity mission, think again. As ever, you have to pay for his 'secrets' to success.

Like many of today's multi-level marketing companies, IML does not just rely on the star power of 'get rich' celebrities like Alex; it also specialises in making new ones. In total there are 11 different earnings tiers, from those making an average annual income of $295 a year on level 1 – known as Platinum 150 – to those at the other end of the scale, Chairman 500, who are raking in a staggering $5m. The day at conference when a marketer moves up a rank is treated like a baptism or bar mitzvah, and it was no different for Des at the London regional IML conference in late autumn, when he was unveiled as making the IML rank Chairman 10 and invited to give his inaugural speech.

The full house, seated in the London Bridge Hotel conference room, consisted of an assortment of low-ranking IML members, newbies, wannabes and seasoned veterans. As Des's name was announced by the host, the room lit up as though he was a soldier returning from war or a record-breaking Olympian. He was applauded, high-fived and cheered as he walked out onto the stage like a boxer to a hip-hop soundtrack. 'I just want to start by giving

God all the praise,' he began. Evangelical Christianity is a subtle undercurrent in IML. Its senior influencers regularly praise God and recite the ideas I heard growing up in a Pentecostal church, although what IML had created was a church for FOREX.

Everyone in the room felt a sense of pride in their identity as a so-called trader, even if they had no idea what they were doing. Being a trader had a glamour for this collection of predominantly working-class and ethnic-minority Londoners, regardless of how much money they did or did not make. Since childhood Des had wanted to drive a nice car, wear a nice suit and feel like somebody important. On this day he was the centre of the room. He felt like a king in a fiefdom built around FOREX. Pyramid schemes have often been the most accessible road to so-called riches for those without elite credentials. In the case of people like Des, it is difficult to hate the player when the game is fixed and we are all playing it in one way or another.

Many of the men who make up this world of day traders and aspiring billionaires are like nearly every man I grew up with. Like myself they were raised with an awareness that they were considered a social problem to be solved, and with it a pressure to confound the limitations on their lives. They view their ambition as a rebellion against the status quo, but in signing up to exploitative and speculative schemes that add no value and solve no problems, they are only reinforcing it. No double-breasted jacket, supercar or Louis Vuitton bag can mask the reality that in taking from the down-and-out, those who could be considered winners are even more tragic than the losers.

8

BLACK LIVES MATTER, HERE'S MY CA$H APP

'Bro, you heard of Twitter?' At the age of 20, I knew nothing about the site, but unbeknownst to my friend, he was about to put a crack pipe to my fingertips. I set up an account on 26 March 2009 in the SOAS library. 'It's mad, bro, you can speak to celebrities,' Kofi said, although what he did not say was that Twitter would make me and millions of others feel like one. Over the next decade, after thousands of mundane daily decrees to my meagre following, I watched the platform mutate from a jovial personalised newswire into an all-powerful villain assailing public decency and democracy.

Although the app has given me and 187 million other daily followers the power to wrestle what the world talks about away from a handful of old rich white men, being able to demand attention at will has changed us. The app's ability to reward us with applause when we say something witty, cogent or urgent has led us to modify our way of life online. Offline, most of us try to evade conflict, but on Twitter it is relished as an opportunity to flex our intelligence for the attention of whatever group we are trying to impress in the pursuit of 'clout'. In this effort to present the best version of ourselves, we have become our worst, and created a new form of influencer wearing activist clothing.

Despite the belief that Twitter has enabled progressive activism, a big casualty of clout rage has arguably been digital social justice movements for racial and gender equality, most visibly expressed via hashtags like #BlackLivesMatter and #MeToo. Influencers masquerading as activists have hijacked progressive social movements, distorted their truths for their own financial gain and even engaged in outright fabrication. These influencers have managed to divorce activism from collective action and turned it into self-serving individual branding. Their end goal is not social change that benefits others, but a cheque, and if possible, a cult-like following they can also cash in on.

One of the internet's biggest trendsetters has been 'Black Twitter', the collective of English-speaking black social media users from North America, Europe and Afropolitan cities like Nairobi and Abuja. Black Twitter is made up of millions of Twitter users trading in-jokes, insults, and commentary about everything from Western foreign policy to reality television. It is driven by the same combative, sound-system mic culture that has defined hip-hop and grime. Witty users are rewarded for the best comebacks and 'hot takes' with retweets. A severe and burning retort is known as a 'dragging'.

The nature of internet echo chambers is that viral events that engage millions can remain underground and unseen to millions of others. Black Twitter is decentralised, with untold local, regional and interest subsections, such as the derogatorily named 'Gucci belt' Twitter, a term used to describe the sub-working class so enamoured with wealth and conservative ideas on gender that they post pictures in Gucci belts and other ostentatious fashions whilst sparring online over questions as deep as who pays on a first date, is eating ass acceptable, should men give women an allowance and what is too high a sexual 'body count' for a woman. However, the most sophisticated and era-defining event on Black Twitter remains the Black Lives Matter (BLM) movement, a decentralised digital protest led by queer black women at a time when the internet helped them to find both a voice and each other.

Black Lives Matter started as a Facebook post by activist Alicia Garza. In 2013, Alicia was a graduate of both the University of California and San Francisco State University. She was educated, upwardly mobile, a trade union organiser and part of a burgeoning new wave of progressive black digital natives caught in the paradox of President Obama's second term. His election was hailed as the beginning of a post-racial American meritocracy where ethnicity was no longer a bar. However, as much as many wanted this to be true, America was still a nation unable to escape its origins of racial hierarchy and violence. A year earlier, in 2012, unarmed 17-year-old Trayvon Martin had been shot dead in Florida by George Zimmerman, a man almost twice his age, who was stalking him on the grounds that the minor appeared suspicious. The killing was widely compared to the racist lynching of 14-year-old African American Emmett Till in Mississippi 50 years earlier. Zimmerman claimed he was standing his ground and was acquitted of murder.

Trayvon's death was yet another chapter in a long history of violence against black Americans not afforded state protection in life or justice in death. It prompted Alicia to go on Twitter to pen what she called 'a love letter to black people': 'The sad part is, there's a section of America who is cheering and celebrating right now, and that makes me sick to my stomach. We GOTTA get it together y'all. Stop saying we are not surprised. That's a damn shame in itself. I continue to be surprised at how little black lives matter. And I will continue that. Stop giving up on black life. Black people, I love you. I love us. Our lives matter.'

After Alicia pressed the send button, her Facebook friend Patrisse Cullors turned the key passage into a hashtag, #BlackLivesMatter. But it was not until a police officer shot and killed an 18-year-old Missouri teenager named Michael Brown in 2014 that it exploded into the most significant American movement since Occupy and became a household mantra. Today, #BlackLivesMatter has been shared over 50 million times, with over 30 million on Instagram alone. Online protest led to offline protests in Ferguson, and the hashtag was used to spread information and organise bus rides to join the front line. As Ferguson erupted into fierce clashes with heavy-handed authorities, the whole world watched it live in tweets and video streams posted to social media, sharing and resharing. The movement had gone viral.

Both Patrisse and Alicia were experienced organisers and activists in the black LGBTQ community, and set up BLM as an official organisation with chapters across North America and even the UK, though most internet users merely used the hashtag to express their anger rather than to take part in any formal organisation. While African Americans have existed with a deep awareness of racial violence, most white Americans have preferred wilful ignorance, with the aid of a historically biased media. But the ubiquity of smartphones and a culture where we record every part of our life has forced America to consistently witness itself for the first time. #BlackLivesMatter is the result. It has become the conduit through which horrific videos of police violence against African Americans have been seen across the world, with the slogan embraced especially in multiracial post-colonial societies in Latin America and western Europe with historic racial inequalities. Through the #BlackLivesMatter hashtag we have watched policemen shoot an innocent child, aim their guns at schoolgirls, threaten young women with death, fatally choke an unarmed father and kill in cold blood.

The problem is that merely sharing the videos feels like activism for some internet users when in reality it is merely gratuitous consumption. Videos of death are treated like just another form of content. In the past, raising awareness was a first step of activism, but for influencers it is the only stage. In recent years, millions with an eye on their own following have commonly shared videos of violence and added their own caption to ensure they do not miss the chance of their angry tweet going viral. In some cases victims have even become useful memes or caption punchlines to mask self-interested ambition as altruism. No victim of police violence has been memeified like Breonna Taylor, who was shot dead in her sleep by intruding police officers. The #JusticeForBreonna hashtag has been used as constant garnish for self-promoters, although few as brazen as when the actor and influencer Lili Reinhart, with 28.2

million followers, posted a topless picture of herself sitting on a beach with the caption: 'Now that my sideboob has gotten your attention, Breonna Taylor's murderers have not been arrested. Demand justice.' Reinhart apologised when the internet recoiled, but she was far from the only one using Taylor's murder so crassly.[1]

The US civil rights movement has lionised its biggest characters. Figures from Harriet Tubman to Martin Luther King are now immortalised in global memory. Although the founders of BLM preferred a flatter structure for the organisation than many of its forerunners, that is not the way social media is set up to work. Twitter is designed to create hierarchies. The aim is to build a following with your voice at the centre, and the unwritten rule is to have far more followers than you are following – a model that is more likely to build celebrity than an egalitarian community. Unsurprisingly, #BlackLivesMatter created just that: a generation of superstar activist influencers, none bigger than DeRay Mckesson. While the movement's founders, Alicia and Patrisse, have grown their large Twitter followings to 100,000 and 65,000 respectively, DeRay's following currently stands at over a million. At present, of the 10 people the megastar Beyoncé follows, DeRay is one.

While all the leading voices in America's new civil rights movement are articulate and telegenic, DeRay captured the limelight with a talent for sound bites, succinct oratory and being at the heart of the story. Then 29 and working as an administrator in Baltimore, he travelled to Ferguson, where by design or accident he became a full-time protester and a celebrity activist reporting from the scene to a growing audience on Twitter. He was a BLM activist who was never quite part of BLM. Nevertheless, he was anointed as such by international media to play the role of spokesperson. He did it well and to much applause from ordinary African Americans.

DeRay has become a fixture on celebrity shows like *The Late Show*, been named one of *Time* magazine's 30 most influential people on the internet, and is a regular on the A-list party scene. At *Vanity Fair*'s prestigious Oscars party, he was on brand in his trademark blue Patagonia puffer vest over his tuxedo alongside Janelle Monáe, Gabrielle Union and Donald Glover. However, in recent years the influencer has become a figure of scrutiny among many civilian activists. When promoting his book *On the Other Side of Freedom*, he even found himself the subject of protests. He had put himself at the forefront of communities who now accused him of parachuting in for media glory and using police brutality to build a name on the lucrative speaking circuit. There were also queries about his relationship with Big Tech.

DeRay became a brand ambassador for Twitter in all but name. He wore T-shirts promoting the site, and publicly trialled and promoted the company's new streaming service. Although he denied being paid to tweet, his gushing praise of Twitter raised eyebrows. In 2014, he publicly and profusely thanked the company's founders: 'In many ways, you saved our lives and allowed us to fight for the lives of others by creating Twitter. Thank you #Ferguson.' In hindsight these thanks were premature, as the platform also enabled the far right and allowed Donald Trump to lie, troll and abuse his way into the White House. Trump even used the site as a de facto executive tool of government.

In recent years, DeRay has found himself in a Twitter beef with a civil rights influencer even more prolific and maligned than himself, and with even more followers. Former pastor Shaun King has gone viral sharing videos of violence against African Americans, becoming one of Twitter's most prominent citizen journalists, and is arguably the only other new digital influencer to rival DeRay's internet celebrity. Even Cardi B has hailed him as a hero.[2] On the night King was recognised for his work by the pop star Rihanna, DeRay penned a letter accusing him of being a scammer, misappropriating funds raised for civil rights campaigns, false claims and profiteering from other activists' work.[3] King responded with his own editorial highlighting a 72-page audit he claimed exonerated him, and pointed to the Ferguson activists who accused DeRay of the same thing.[4] The entertainment website The Grio called the beef 'a pissing match between two men who are trying to claim a throne neither necessarily deserves'.[5]

Samaria Rice, the mother of Tamir Rice, a 12-year-old shot dead in 2014 by police officers whilst playing in the park, publicly criticised the leading activists of BLM for 'monopolising and capitalising' on her family's fight for justice.[6] She named King and Tamika Mallory in particular. Mallory, who has gained over 1.1 million followers as an influencer activist, was also criticised for taking money to be part of a corporate promotion campaign for the car manufacturer Cadillac. This backlash against influencer activism even engulfed one of the founders of BLM itself. In 2020, Patrisse Cullors was asked to explain how she had built a private million-dollar property portfolio generated from her new-found position at the helm of a civil rights movement whilst publicly proclaiming socialist values.[7]

On social media, the leading activists are set up more like private enterprises, with their own huge fan base of followers who buy into their brands. DeRay, King and Mallory all launched high-profile media careers from a hashtag none of them created. The infighting between the most prominent figures attached to #BlackLivesMatter has become a lesson in how social media incentivises competition and disincentivises collectivism. It is also a lesson in how the mobilising power of a hashtag can be launched for professional and personal ambition disguised as altruism, a lesson learnt by every wannabe guru and opportunist in the ecosystem.

In 2020, what was effectively the lynching of George Floyd by Minneapolis city police triggered a reaction so visceral that institutions everywhere had to reassess their racist legacies. For the first time in my life, a real conversation was being had, but within collective actions there were individual attempts to profiteer, as millions looked for causes to donate to. In London, a cohort that included black beauty bloggers, entrepreneurs and influencers set up a GoFundMe page that cited George Floyd's death as a motivation, promising to reward those doing racial justice work in the UK. However, the initial money raised was for their individual pockets.

Black Twitter has been defined as much by protest as it has by its cultural influence. Mining Black Twitter for media has made companies millions and created what many users see as a new form of work. Grammar, phrases and jokes created by black Twitter users have been appropriated by multinational companies for advertising campaigns. In 2019, the popular American fast-food chain Popeyes launched its new chicken sandwich with a social media campaign that used black colloquial language to publicly ridicule its rival Wendy's by quoting Wendy's tweet about its new burger, 'Y'all good?'[8] It was a gesture that was the equivalent of digital beef as their new chicken burgers went head to head.

Hundreds of thousands of people have shared the tweets and cheered on the flamboyant voice that sent Popeyes viral. The company shortly after announced that their new sandwich had sold out almost everywhere. The demand was so high that the restaurant and social media users reported standstill queues, exhausted workers and a shortage of burgers that lasted up to two months. The attention generated by the single tweet was estimated to be worth $65m.[9]

In addition to the clear commercial strength of Black Twitter, words like 'squad' and 'bae' and phrases like 'on fleek' and 'yas queen' have become part of popular American culture and multicultural London English. The ironic black expression 'woke' has even become ubiquitous in mainstream media, albeit as the most misappropriated, misused and misunderstood word of the decade.

Black Twitter's cultural influence on internet grammar is second to none, and although the ethics of publicly shared culture being harnessed for private profit is much disputed, that has not stopped its biggest critics from participating in the competition to go viral through wit and wordplay. Black Twitter has become a factory of internet writers and watchful plagiarists hoping to find micro-internet fame by typing punchy prose, or copying and pasting it from somebody else's page. The ambition to grow a following that can be indirectly monetised through television appearances, speaking gigs and book deals has become far more direct. Underneath viral tweets, Twitter users post affiliate links to products they receive commission on, and increasingly more users set up Cash App accounts and link them to their most viral threads or tweets.

The app allows other users to transfer you money if they like your tweets. The consequence has been to turn online communities into vicious competitions for attention and private gain. This goes beyond Black Twitter but looks even more dishonest in a community that is striving for equality. Twitter rewards not only the most articulate but also those who pander to their audience's most extreme biases. The platform's 280-character limit is not the best for conveying nuance, but it is the economic incentives that have turned it into a race to the bottom. Twitter is not a place to expect honest descriptions about the world when those making them do so for applause and attention irrespective of whether they believe in what they are saying.

The most tribal of Twitter's communities are drawn up along the lines of race, gender and partisan political allegiance, because those are often the most emotive and easiest ways to antagonise. Each week a new 'race row' grips tabloid programmes like the UK's *Good Morning Britain* (*GMB*). The programme and its former host Piers Morgan have discussed whether concern over racist language is itself racist, defended British colonialism whilst guests pointed out Britain's former use of concentration camps, and told a black guest he should repatriate himself if he believes Britain has a racism problem.[10] *GMB* purposely chooses to inflame rather than inform its viewers to gain newspaper column inches, and it regularly surfs Twitter looking for the next outrage to mine for its audience. Sometimes it feels like everyone on the platform is doing the same.

Secure the bag

Chidera Eggerue is one of the most successful influencers to transcend Black Twitter and become a bona fide mega-influencer, accruing half a million followers after going viral. On 17 July 2017, the former student of the famous BRIT School for Performing & Creative Arts stitched a series of bikini pictures of herself into an online animated GIF, uploaded it to Twitter and repurposed the #BlackLivesMatter format for her own ends. #SaggyBoobsMatter was accompanied by a blog about once desiring a boob job and now rejecting the male gaze. Whereas #BlackLivesMatter tapped into a deep sense of injustice #SaggyBoobsMatter was a hashtag Chidera used to post bikini shots and braless thirst traps, and to encourage other women to do the same without worrying about whether their breasts fitted the conventional standard of attractiveness.

As Instagram made self-objectification ordinary, Chidera's gesture declared that every woman should have the right to participate regardless of whether they met popular beauty standards. Her campaign was a dream for the tabloids, merging as it did their interests in controversy and women's bodies. The BuzzFeed report on her alone hit over a million clicks. Chidera signed to the newly launched agency Diving Bell, which had a roster of high-profile activist influencers, and her celebrity soared. The British Nigerian was hailed as the 'mastermind' of a new movement by glossy magazines even if #SaggyBoobsMatter was part of a long-term noticeable trend about body image.[11] Leading model Ashley Graham and the Curve pin-up Denise Bidot launched, respectively, #IAmSizeSexy and #ThereIsNoWrongWayToBeAWoman with the moral that 'all women can be beautiful'. The hashtags they promote are part of a protest against the edited pictures that force an impossible aesthetic on women, reinforcing the idea that their value is tied to how they look. Graham is a supermodel who has covered the exalted swimsuit issue of *Sports Illustrated* and yet has become the face of a social movement representing marginalised bodies that the world considers undesirable.

If body positivity appears to be a kickback against brands selling an impossible and unhealthy image of womanhood to drive sales in the $500bn beauty industry, in reality it has become another vehicle of consumption. Despite influencers like Graham being described as starting a 'beauty revolution',[12] models like her are businesswomen in activist clothing selling a message that suits consumerism: anyone can be beautiful and feel good wearing sexy products that just by chance those models are promoting.

The body positive movement has historically centred on women who were fat, dark-skinned, disabled or all three, to help them feel comfortable in their bodies when mass advertising suggested that to be beautiful was to be their opposite. In contrast, at the helm of this new body positive movement are curvaceous and traditionally beautiful models who call themselves activists but operate more like private enterprises. The most high profile do not unite behind a single campaign like environmentalists or other political campaigners. Instead, each model has launched their own campaign, had their slogan copyrighted and turned it into merchandise. Ordinary women are encouraged to take risqué pictures and promote them using the various models' hashtags as a form of protest, yet most prominent hashtag campaigns are incorporated trademarks that make their owners an income. The irony is these hashtags are orchestrated by conventionally attractive men and women.

Chidera herself is photogenic, with desirable proportions. Her social media page is one long magazine editorial. In pictures she is fierce, fun and commanding like any other professional model. Chidera and her PR have repackaged her decision not to wear a bra as ground-breaking, even though the gesture first made headlines in 1968, when feminist campaigners famously removed and burned their bras to campaign against the Miss America beauty pageant. In contrast, Chidera removed hers to encourage women to take part in the new digital beauty contest happening on Instagram. From there, her platform has boomed and she is now sought out as an expert on everything from racial equality and public safety to women's self-care. In the process, she has become one of the new 'activist influencers' deploying a template that an uncountable number of young women and men are now copying.

What makes Chidera so successful is not just the size of her online following. The influencer, better known by her internet personality the Slumflower, does not have millions of followers like a *Love Island* contestant, tens of millions of subscribers like a blue-chip YouTuber, or even a fan base of cult black influencers like the controversial Chakabars, who has acquired more than a million predominantly black Instagram followers from posting memes, topless thirst traps from his gym workouts, and vaccine misinformation. In comparison, what gives Chidera much of her digital clout is the make-up of her following. In the world of internet work, the so-called influencers who have built a devoted fan base from relative obscurity usually belong to one of several tribes: fashionista, campaigner, advice guru, specialist blogger, body inspiration, prosperity prophet or model. The Slumflower is all seven, and has a broad commercial appeal. Organisations she has fronted campaigns for include the democratic socialist (kinda) Mayor of London and the multinational corporate brand Adidas.

Unlike many internet influencers, Chidera's online following actually translates offline, a feat I witnessed at her debut live show in Hackney. On a stormy night just before COVID hit in 2020, the queue spanned across an entire block. When Chidera appeared later than advertised, the crowd erupted into applause as she moved around the stage exuding infectious charisma, wearing a figure-hugging white dress and pink high heels wrapped to her ankles with a ribbon and bow. The soundtrack to her entrance was empowerment stripper anthem 'Beef FloMix' by the young trap rapper Flo Milli, which opens: 'I like cash and my hair to my ass (I do) / Do the dash, can you make it go fast? (Go, go) / Fuck the fame, all I want is them bands (Money) / If she keep on muggin', I'ma steal her man (I got him).'

The song was a sign of things to come, even if it didn't quite match the audience. Inside the shabby-chic arts centre was a crowd of up to 1,000 women that appeared to be 90 per cent white. Chidera's audience had shifted from when she first started out. One PR company that has worked with her told me this had made her more appealing to major brands and allowed her to gain higher-paid opportunities than black influencers with three times her following – at least if theirs were made up mostly of black women. More significantly, Chidera's online following are decision makers; they are young women who are newspaper section editors, artists, curators, TV directors, senior producers, corporate lawyers, businesswomen, senior publishers and writers. She has actual influence. Many are millennials, with power in the industries that shape British public life. Millennials are the biggest consumer group, and millennial women are the biggest spenders, whether single or partnered.[13] It is this consumer group that brands and companies are desperate to capture. Anyone with their ear has genuine power.

At her first live show, Chidera was hailed like the second coming of Christ. 'I'm in the mood to have a church-style environment and share some testimonies,' she said as she called on pre-prepared guests to share how she and her good book had changed their lives. 'How did you take your power back?' she asked them. To this crowd of predominantly white women between the ages of 18 and 30 – and in some cases older – she was an aspirational figure, a guru happy to teach them how to get over bad boyfriends and be a general 'bad bitch' like her.

Chidera's early following had appeared to consist mainly of black and brown women. On Twitter she had regularly condemned white women's theft of black culture, but she had since switched up her act to include those who proved to be the most lucrative. She had tweeted that 'white women wanna be us so bad' and told Twitter, 'I talk about the problem of white women imitating black women whilst oppressing them,' yet here she was entertaining a white crowd for payment in the same manner as a hip-hop artist condemning white fans for saying the N-word whilst being happy to take their money.

Chidera's provocative Slumflower persona has built a cult following of those who both love her and hate her, which has helped to raise her star power. The Slumflower has been hailed as a black feminist icon by white feminist writers in magazines from *Vogue* to *Dazed*, despite her message being convoluted and contrarian. She told the room that 'modern feminism is ruining your life,' considers men who are their child's primary caregiver 'losers' and channels the spirit of Margaret Thatcher in the packaging of Pam Grier's Foxy Brown. The journalist Ash Sarkar described her philosophy as 'intersectional Thatcherism'.[14] Chidera tells women to only date affluent men and take anything you can. Ask them to pay your bills, buy you designer clothes or provide an allowance, she says.

Chidera provides a real-life version of the internet sensation Joanne the Scammer, a fictional character created by a then twenty-something named Branden Miller, who describes herself as 'a liar, a scammer. I love robbery and fraud. I'm a messy bitch who lives for drama.' The act went viral as the embodiment of a generation who grew up on hip-hop desperate to get rich and enjoy an affluent life at the expense of male sponsors. Joanne currently has 1.7 million followers on Instagram, but whereas she is an ironic comedic persona, Chidera always stays in character. 'If a man walks his way into my life, I will squeeze every last coin out of him and send him on his way,' she tweeted. She considers it to be reparations, a term she appropriated from the campaign to compensate the descendants of transatlantic slavery for the generational inequalities that have followed.

Chidera posts rants against capitalism while promoting its most predatory values and laughing at those who are economically disadvantaged. She accused black British men, who are one of only two groups where the gender pay gap is reversed,[15] of holding back successful black women because of their lack of economic might. 'I'm NOT dying poor in the name of black men of all people,' she tweeted, taking the Conservative position that they needed to pull themselves up by the bootstraps. 'Stop coddling black men,' she warned. 'As an ex social justice mule, I can tell you that most of us are driven by the GUILT of "leaving

black men behind" even though black men as a system-
atic cohort do NOT reciprocate the undeserved loyalty.
LEAVE THESE PEOPLE WHERE THEY AT' and 'let
these people compete for US'.

Appealing to all women, Chidera positioned herself as a
relationship guru and began dispensing advice to the thousands of young women who sought it. In one case a girl
got in touch claiming to be dating a man studying to be
a doctor who loved her, paid for dates when he could and
treated her 'amazingly', but his two-year medical masters
now meant splitting the bill more regularly than she liked.
She asked Slumflower, 'Have I set the foundation we split
everything forever?' Slumflower's response was her default:
dump him, sis. 'Get a new boyfriend. There are richer,
cuter, more successful, funnier, more romantic, far more
interesting guys out there if you widen your network,' she
told her. This was one of her more moderate positions.

Chidera's contradictions have been regularly criticised.
She has tweeted that the only way to protect women is
for men to be wiped out. She also posted a retort against
women who care about the societal pressures that push
men to commit suicide. 'I don't have time to think about
the reasons why the system you created at my expense to
benefit you is now choking you … If men are committing
s*icide because they can't cry, how's it my concern?'[16] When
the *Guardian* writer Zoe Williams suggested her position

lacked humanity, Williams was lambasted by influencers who suggested it was inappropriate for a white woman to speak out against a black woman, despite Chidera being unquestionably the more influential figure. In the past, Chidera had tweeted an article about 'how white women use strategic tears to avoid accountability'; now she herself was doing the same thing while regularly displaying her new-found privileges.

Newly minted from high-paying campaigns, she told her audience of young women that they could only truly know themselves by living alone, despite that being an impossible dream in the British capital for any of her listeners earning the average salary. Even when some of her own followers questioned this advice, and queried how wise it was to tell young women to judge a man by his bank balance because it could make them prone to exploitation, Chidera tweeted that 'White women and black men enjoy policing the financial desires of black women because the lot of you deeply believe black women shouldn't dare demand the highest of treatment. Some of us aren't looking for musty struggle soulmates.'

This deflection is not unique to Chidera. The academic Emma Dabiri in her best-selling essay *What White People Can Do Next* writes how influencers presenting themselves as activists have misappropriated identity politics to avoid accountability for their own commercial gain:

The very nature of social media, particularly platforms like Twitter, rewards outrage, by amassing followers, likes and retweets from both the like-minded and the cowed. Online commentators remain in 'angry' setting … When 'activism' is bound up in capital relations, and your Twitter persona is your brand, where is the incentive for the recognition of affinity, of solidarity across once artificially imposed lines (identities)? Technology, which promised to liberate us, and which has undeniably contributed to gains for individual women, ethnic minorities and LGBTQ+ people, is a beast of paradox.

Chidera's persona cemented her position as a pantomime villain of Black Twitter, but her callous words on male mental health led many of her peers to fear that brands would no longer work with her. Some said that she had 'fumbled the bag' of money she could make. Several began to reach out privately, offering support and advice, but Chidera did not like being told what to do or that she was in the wrong. She told them to kick rocks and broke contact. Soon more visible black influencers, albeit with far less influence, began to publicly rebuke her brand of hyper-individualism. But there was no sign of Chidera being blacklisted for her statement, though the backlash did lead to her deleting her tweet.

In reality, brands have little value beyond their profit line, and Slumflower's extreme positioning only sent her more viral. The polarisation also led her most devout followers to fiercely defend her, and even as a critical mass of prominent black British women turned on her, she still had a hardcore following of young white women who connected with her broad message to be selfish. 'You come first! And that's a double entendre,' she told her audience in Hackney, sticking out her tongue and shimmying to delighted laughter. 'You need to be militant with your happiness.'

The event was part of her campaign to push her book *How to Get Over a Boy*. The volume is notably low on text, just like her best-selling debut, *What a Time to Be Alone*. At times, only two or three words appear on a page, with the rest taken up with youthful colours, illustrations and patterns. It is a self-help book that is low on actual self-help. Despite that, both books have been widely covered by the literati, and feature heavily on credible recommended-read lists published in magazines like *Elle*. Chidera's place among the British elite was cemented when she was invited to guest-edit Radio 4's flagship *Today* programme, a show that at the time had no black presenters or reporters, and which reportedly numbers the Queen among its listeners.

Now here in Hackney she was teaching impressionable young white women how to use sex to get what they wanted.

'I like to call it the bad bitch mentality,' she laughed on an evening where she was undoubtedly the queen bee.

Chidi, as she calls herself for short, is a phenomenon. Despite weathering Twitter storms, and her fans weathering real ones to see her live, she is an unqualified success. This is not an ephemeral community like Black Twitter, but an actual fan base, ironically built from appropriating the success of the hashtag that brought Black Twitter to mainstream attention.

Despite the personal ambition behind #SaggyBoobsMatter, the movement itself has a simple message that is positive and relatable. It was when Slumflower began to rebrand herself as an internet relationship guru that she pivoted into a more problematic persona. She was pulled into the world of relationship finessers, communities of young women who discuss ways to make money out of men, though paradoxically, it's the paying customers – other women – of these gurus who make them rich. Chidera became an unofficial apprentice of an underground African-American 'dating coach' named Imani Yvonne, who claimed her clients were having success with rich men following her tips on how to find them and fleece them. Although Chidera admitted to being a client of Yvonne, the two formed a friendship of equals, collaborated on videos and holidayed together. After following Yvonne online, Chidera became increasingly more overt in her pursuit of material wealth and began to model herself on her mentor.

Her publisher Quadrille, buoyed by the success of her first book, commissioned a second, targeted at heartbroken young women. In the build-up to the book, Chidera released a series of videos and posts encouraging young women to be transactional with sex and even to seek a living allowance in return for their time. 'I'm always making sure that I look like a goddess because I want to be treated like one,' she said. In a U-turn from the moral of #SaggyBoobsMatter, she even encouraged young women to dress attractively to get the attention of the right men. 'If you don't have enough money to constantly update your wardrobe you can revamp what you have … find ways if you're really really sure about what you want for yourself, don't let anyone talk you out of this because they're not gonna be with you when you're in the later years of your life wishing that you used your 20s or your 30s or your 40s differently.'

Imani Yvonne would later accuse Chidera of ripping off her hustle. Chidera's book is too broad-brush and low on advice to be considered plagiarism, but Yvonne claimed that she had taken her advice and repackaged it as her own. In the past, Chidera had publicly praised and directed followers towards Yvonne, but the American felt her apprentice had not kept paying her dues and was slowly erasing her from the picture. Ironically, Chidera would soon accuse a rival influencer with more clout of doing exactly the same.

Twenty-one-year-old Florence Given had made her name on Instagram illustrating sharable feminist memes, accruing over half a million followers. Her brand of introductory feminism won plaudits, notably from Chidera herself, who publicly endorsed her – until Florence's sales surpassed her own. In 2020, Given made history as the youngest author to spend consecutive weeks in the top five of the *Sunday Times* Bestseller List. Her book, *Women Don't Owe You Pretty*, made up of memoir, pop feminist messaging and her own illustrations, was a huge hit after a meticulous social media marketing campaign. She did all the things white feminists are told they should: she 'checked her privilege', recognising where her experience of womanhood differed from that of more marginalised women; and she credited Chidera and a number of black feminist writers for their influence, even though Chidera's book was hardly black feminist scholarship.

Yet Chidera accused Florence of copying her book, and attributed her success to 'white supremacy', pointing to the long history of black artists having their style copied to the benefit of white artists – as in the case of rock and roll. Given's book is unquestionably in the same genre as Chidera's, written for those who prefer not to read. And although there is truth to the claim that her race made her more marketable to white consumers, she not only credited Chidera's influence in the first place, but the two women were of equal status and popularity. Chidera was signed to a major publishing house first, achieved a best-selling book first, and at present cannot be considered a marginalised voice.

Chidera then told her followers that because she had spoken out, the manager she shared with Florence had dropped her and kept her rival, further proof of white supremacy. Only this was not quite true. In reality, Chidera had severed ties with her manager months earlier and was serving out a three-month notice period at the time of the fallout. She had effectively resigned, but told her followers she had been fired to generate a grievance around a fictional iniquity.

Given, who appeared in awe of Chidera, posted: 'I care about Chidera a lot, she was my friend, I've supported and shared her work and books on my platform for years. She absolutely has inspired me, and she is credited multiple times throughout my book. Chidera's pain and where it comes from is entirely valid, conversations about race and privilege are always necessary ...' If she thought this would appease Chidera, she was wrong; it only drove her on. Chidera continued her campaign, telling her followers: 'This is white supremacy at work and in real time, you are watching a black woman being pushed to the back in her own liberation movement.' Privately, many of Chidera's black peers disagreed, but publicly they remained silent as her sycophants rallied around her. Most appeared to be white, and were no doubt conscious of their own image and fearful of being told to check their privilege.

Chidera's attitude would puzzle anyone who has worked in academia, where everyone is desperate for their research to be shared, cited, and reproduced with credit. If she really cared about the ideas she championed, Florence's success in getting over 100,000 people to buy into feminist values would have been hers too. The problem is that Chidera's work is not activism; it is private enterprise for private gain and fame.

At one point at the Hackney event, the stage was almost mobbed when the Slumflower invited members of the audience up to speak. What was notable about each of the women who came up was how vulnerable they sounded despite their range of ages and backgrounds. The first woman to arrive on stage introduced herself as Becky. She had broken up with her boyfriend and was adjusting to singledom. Forty-two-year-old Roxanne said she had escaped an abusive marriage. Both women had found hope in a charismatic young woman who was still working it all out herself. However, despite emphasising the merits of transactional relationships with men, the truth was that this attitude extended to Chidera's relationship with the women in the room too.

The new internet economy views every relationship as a chance to cash in, and Chidera's online antics embody this philosophy. She regularly posts her PayPal details on her Instagram to encourage her white fans to gift her money as a form of compensation for their privilege, regardless of whether she herself has more of it. If her Instagram stories are accurate, she has made thousands in donations from young white women who said they felt guilty that Given had not paid her 'reparations'. The episode was best captured by the writer Jason Okundaye, who said: 'The thing is Slumflower knows she's not getting any "reparations" from Florence and that she will lose in court [on plagiarism] so this whole campaign really is just to manipulate her followers into sending her more money, buy her work etc. It's not about Florence at all.'

The new rewards and financial possibilities shaping our behaviour online are changing not just the way we relate to each other but how we relate to reality. When feminist peers first began to ask Chidera to explain her advice and questioned what qualified her to make it, Chidera replied that she did not want to be a model to follow. 'I have NO aspirations of being anybody's "hero", role model or perfect feminist and that's okay,' she tweeted. This is a statement that looks dishonest from someone who actively marketed herself as a guru and invited women to share what she had taught them.

When the Hackney event ended, the room rose to give Chidera a standing ovation. She had pulled off a performance that even seasoned comedians would struggle to manage. She had held the audience's gaze, entertained them and somehow made them love her more than when they had come in. There was a point during proceedings when young women were literally running to the stage for the chance to sit down beside her. Her incoherent mix of Igbo entrepreneurialism, gender conservatism, professional narcissism, consumerism and hyper-individualism wrapped in feminist packaging was both a winner and a work in progress. She was making it up as she went along, like most young adults trying to find their place in the world and working out what they believe in. The difference is that in faking or forcing expertise she does not have, Chidera embodies the emptiness of the social media economy.

After the auditorium emptied, I joined the queue to meet her that wound all the way up the stairwell. I was the penultimate person waiting, clutching a copy of her debut book to be signed. She was as warm and charismatic offstage as on. She opened the book and wrote: 'KEEP SMILING! LOVE, the Slumflower x'.

A thread

Twitter has helped to build the profiles of many social causes, but the way the platform works means the profit motive is never far away. In 2018, a woman calling herself Ashley wrote 30 tweets in the mould of Slumflower. The aim of her thread was to appeal to and empower women. 'You ever see a girl in denial about being in a toxic relationship and want to grab her by her face and tell her how much better her life will be once she comes to her senses? That shit is the absolute worst to just stand by and watch after you've been through it all yourself …'

She then tweeted about being coerced and bullied by an emotionally abusive boyfriend, and posted pictures and video of the impact the relationship had had on her weight. This segued into a woman talking about a weight-loss programme. The thread was seen by tens of millions of Twitter users, was shared over 83,000 times and liked more than 300,000 times by those standing in solidarity against abuse and for women's empowerment. However, it transpired it was all a fraud. The pictures posted had been stolen from a cam girl and the video from a YouTuber. The thread closed with a link to the dietary supplement Therma Trim.[17] It was a scam designed to make money using abuse and empowerment as an emotive ruse to encourage sharing.

False threads and activist social media accounts for profit are rampant all over the platform. There was uproar when the highly followed activist account @feminist, with over 6.5 million followers posting anti-sexist content, was revealed to be run by a private company owned by two men. Jacob Castaldi and Tanner Sweitzer are the millennials behind Contagious Creative, an ad agency 'responsible for creating and managing a network of over 10,000,000 followers of Instagram communities',[18] which included owning the accounts @feminist, @itsfeminism and @march. These feminist meme platforms were accused by digital creator Sam Sedlack of obscuring their male ownership and stealing the work of activists.[19] Like all aggregator pages, the accounts repost other people's content. In their case, it's from female influencers and illustrators with smaller followings. This is just one example of men trying to go viral by performing womanhood.

The Twitter account @emoblackthot had over 170,000 followers. She was a personality in the community of black female influencers who promoted self-care and body positivity aimed at black women. She was Twitter famous in the thriving community of queer black women, where she spoke about her struggles with period cramps and would ask followers for financial support when times got hard by posting her Cash App details. Her burgeoning internet celebrity led many to speculate on who was behind the account. Some black women even reasoned that it was the stealth account of icon Rihanna. @emoblackthot chose the music magazine *Paper* to make the big reveal: Isaiah Hickland, a 23-year-old African-American man, was the mind behind the female persona. Black Twitter was stunned.

If the unveiling of @emoblackthot sent ripples through a niche corner of Black Twitter, the community's greatest and most telling fraud was perpetrated by the actor Jussie Smollett. A TV star who had begun to rebrand himself as a visible civil rights activist, he regularly promoted Black Lives Matter, which increased his own stardom. In January 2019, he reported that he had been jumped by two Trump-supporting attackers wearing MAGA hats, who attempted to lynch him. A picture of the bruised actor circulated on Twitter, and #Justice4Jussie began to trend. President Trump's rhetoric had polarised the country, and the attack appeared to demonstrate the tragic consequences of inflaming racial hatred. Leading Democrats and celebrities came out in support of Jussie, and in his first public appearance after the attack, he gave a defiant speech and compared himself to the rapper Tupac.

However, there was suspicion over the accuracy of his testimony, and a month later, the actor was charged with filing a false report after two brothers claimed they had been paid to help him with the hoax.[20] The internet was now wondering if he had faked the incident to use the viral currency of victimhood to propel his fame. In December 2021, Jussie was convicted of five counts of disorderly conduct for making fake police reports. There are enough real injustices to report, but in a world where hashtags are effectively cashtags, social media is incentivising dishonesty in more ways than one, and encouraging us to perform activism for money, attention or both.

When I first signed up to Twitter, I was a young idealist actively involved in student campaigns. I used the app like everyone else did. I reshared articles on matters that outraged me, tweeted support for the issues I cared about, and felt validated when people liked what I said. I reposted the tweets of those I agreed with and fiercely debated those I did not, but most of the people I tweeted used the platform in good faith. Today, it feels like the rewards of bad faith have changed Twitter's culture and helped dishonesty to thrive among activists, politicians and even journalists desperate for clout. This has polluted both online and offline public debate.

Twitter has become the location where the first draft of history is written and where the discourse that informs our civic institutions is set. However, just as newspapers have tailored the truths they report on to appeal to the biases of their consumers, ordinary citizens are doing the same to position themselves as influencers with elaborate performances of outrage. As Twitter introduces plans to allow us to be tipped and paid for our tweets, this performance for attention is likely to intensify. The more Twitter has increased its hold on public life, the more public life has descended into dishonesty, and the main winners have been the platform's shareholders. Everyone else is losing.

CONCLUSION

WE ARE ALL INFLUENCERS NOW

In 1968, pop artist Andy Warhol famously wrote that 'in the future everyone will be famous for 15 minutes.' This quote may have become a cliché, but what Warhol probably did not anticipate was quite how momentary attention would become a way of life for hundreds of millions of people. Platforms like Instagram and TikTok have disrupted the old expectations of the working class that they would spend their life in menial work and enabled a new class altogether: celebrity.

In the past, enduring celebrity was a small realm that only a charmed few entered, but nowadays a 'celebrity', according to the UK Advertising Standards Authority, is anyone with 30,000 followers online.[1] Instagram grants you privileged account features with just 10,000 followers. The social media site has over a billion users, and the majority of those who have upgraded to a special business profile designed for influencers, which enables special features like analytics, have between 10,000 and a million followers.[2] Even I have run one of these accounts for my book club. If celebrity was once uncommon or fleeting, these figures reveal that it is now ordinary and mundane. Anyone can now be famous for far longer than 15 minutes.

This promise arguably coincides with the end of the traditional working-class sense of self. The sensibility of millennial and Gen Z adults born to working- and lower-middle-class families in the 1980s and 1990s has shifted. Whereas our parents often accepted their place within Britain's social and economic hierarchy, we now all believe we can make it to the apex.

In making the world smaller, social media has promised to make the possibilities in our lives bigger. Every time we follow the rich and famous, we are invited to take a seat at their table. It is unsurprising that when we see how the 1 per cent live in real time, we increasingly believe that it is possible to join them. However, for many I interviewed in the writing of this book, their road to the top has diverted them into pyramid schemes and get-quick-rich traps. While it's tempting to write them off as naïve, many more of us have taken a more conventional route, only to be crowded out by the competition.

A university education was supposed to be the road to social mobility, but as the supply of graduates has increased, social media has stepped in even here. Graduates are encouraged to build a name for themselves or cultivate a professional identity on social media that makes them stand out. In journalism, that has encouraged those desperate for work to create an exaggerated media identity on sites like Twitter or Clubhouse. For those trying to make it in the world of business, LinkedIn has become the default way to be hired, by curating a conscientious and thoughtful professional identity one humble-brag and business proverb at a time.

On LinkedIn, the start-up kings are the most popular influencers, and the platforms they set up are the hot companies that everyone wants to work for in the hope it will make them rich when they cash out their stock options. In the past decade, the start-up industry has boomed, with investors seeking to pump money into millennials who look the part: curating a persona on social media is their first step to doing so. Whether you are trying to make money from social media or attract money through it, it is now increasingly unclear where influencer culture begins and start-up culture ends, exemplified by a burgeoning new class of highly followed entrepreneurs who straddle celebrity. Yet beneath our generation's public self-confidence is a global market economy that is rigged and fuelling fraud. An entire generation has learnt that they cannot beat it so are trying to join it. My friends and I from working-class communities are no different. One even said he would not be satisfied until he got the invite to go to Davos, the zenith of the 1 per cent.

For over 50 years, Davos has hosted the World Economic Forum's annual conference, a party of the powerful and billionaires. Every year, world leaders and the richest people who have ever lived (usually men) descend en masse on the Swiss ski resort for a meeting that only the most privileged can attend. The guest list is invitation only, and includes presidents, popes and pop stars. In 2012, the annual party had an ambience of fear rather than jubilance. Just three years earlier, the financial system had been in the grip of an existential implosion caused by banks issuing mortgage loans to people who could not afford to pay them back. They then traded the debts between each other, without anyone noticing that the vast majority were worthless, until all hell broke loose.

Held to ransom by the prospect of an economic depression more severe than that of the early 1930s, governments declared the banks too big to fail and bailed them out. The US allocated a staggering $700bn[3] to those facing bankruptcy. The UK government spent over £137bn.[4] Both then spent a further $3 trillion[5] and £375bn[6] respectively, buying assets and bonds from at-risk companies owned by the Davos-going elite. Capitalism had had a near-death experience and managed to escape thanks to taxpayers, but that did not mean confidence immediately bounced back, especially once the economic crisis morphed into a political one. In Iceland, protesters brought down the government, and youth unemployment in Greece hit 60 per cent.[7] And that was just the start.

On 17 September 2011, students, newly politicised young adults and veteran leftists poured on Manhattan's financial district to register their anger at how the interests of the most affluent 1 per cent had been fiercely protected by the state. The party of 1,000 protesters built a settlement in nearby Zuccotti Park, where they stayed for months as the dissent grew into a powerful new movement.

Occupy Wall Street was fuelled by the rage against the post-recession malaise that millennials found themselves graduating into. Entry-level jobs in professional industries were slashed, inequality was rising and the generational contract looked broken: millennials were on course to do worse than their parents. I myself graduated in the aftermath of this recession. The new Conservative-led government made public spending cuts their only real ambition, and even though the economy had returned to growth, for my peers born in the late 1980s to early 1990s, the recession never really ended. The availability of quality professional jobs felt limited, and even when we managed to find them, pay in real terms was down. According to the UK's Institute for Fiscal Studies, median wealth for those born in the late

1980s is 20 per cent lower in their early thirties than it was for those born in the 1970s[8] at the same age.[9] Home ownership for millennials in major cities has all but collapsed due to the financial crisis.

Prior to 2008, interest rates in Britain had fluctuated between 3 per cent and 15 per cent over 30 years.[10] This was good for savers and bad for those with mortgages. To stimulate spending after the banking crisis, banks all over the world slashed interest rates to record lows. And there they have stayed. The low interest rates have fuelled huge asset bubbles. In the UK, the value of houses has ballooned by over 350 per cent since 1990,[11] meaning that millions of millennials have been locked out of home ownership unless they have a vast fortune or parental help, and are forced to pay inflated rents to landlords from prior generations. It is unsurprising that many young people across the world have been reconsidering whether capitalism is a system they want to live under, although the irony is that the influencer culture we are all being sucked into by social media platforms is an expansion of this very system. A world where every area of our social lives and relationships is seen as a potential revenue stream.

The scariest thing is that although millennials habitually back political parties and candidates who stand against the current economic status quo – people such as Jeremy Corbyn and Bernie Sanders – there is a nonchalant acceptance that self-interest and dishonesty are inescapable features of the system. The worst effect of this is the lack of consequences for corruption and deception among those with power. If Trump's presidential success was not proof of this in the US, then the reaction to the corruption in Britain's current governing party is. Amidst a fatal pandemic, revelations that government ministers had granted million-pound COVID contracts to their friends and family, and had even been recipients of public money themselves, were greeted with shoulder shrugs. The silent fear is that our lives have become too atomised for collective action beyond tweets, and that we are increasingly on our own. That was also the message of the banking crisis.

Back then, for myself and my peers graduating into a market that did not know what to do with us and no longer guaranteed rewards, what we desired was meaningful work that brought social status and high salaries. The difficulties of this challenge are obvious. The more sophisticated an economy, the more it rewards pointless jobs devoid of any real meaning. Where is the purpose in betting on whether the price of the dollar is going to rise or fall in the afternoon? What is meaningful about marketing poorly produced clothes manufactured for fast-fashion companies by sweatshops paying poverty wages? These are just two of the supposedly aspirational industries for younger millennials caught between unlimited ambition and limited options.

Over the past decade, the labour market has only become more polarised. Low-paid and insecure work in the gig economy, such as Uber driving, has grown, and the jobs at the top have become more specialist and elusive. Diligent but not particularly gifted graduates who would have expected a comfortable entry-level professional job have turned to hustling, enabled by a new infrastructure made up of LinkedIn, amateur awards, exclusive networks and millennial power lists. There are lists for young black millennials, young women, young activists and young entrepreneurs. The media's insatiable hunger for stories of youth success has meant that being a prodigy appears to be the new normal. Reality TV, business influencers and constant status anxiety have caused more young people than ever to feel as if they should be rich, and that if they are not, then they are failing. It is unsurprising that since social media has taken off, anxiety among young adults has exploded. According to researchers from University College London, 8 per cent of young British women between 18 and 24 suffered from anxiety in 2008. By 2018, this figure had risen to 30 per cent.[12] In that time, the figures for young men also doubled and the researchers identified social media as a significant factor with its endless posts curating perfect lives and prodigious achievement. Yet despite the saturation of youth success stories, millionaire millennials are extreme outliers.

Even on the new 30 Under 30 lists, there are ordinary young people with exaggerated influence. Many are directors of companies with no employees, or activists who have never had an impact on policy, all under pressure to present themselves as the real deal. Is it any wonder that imposter syndrome is rife when everyone is encouraged to oversell? One of my university friends successfully applied to be featured on the Forbes list of most influential millennials. When it was announced that he had made the cut, his friends from his neighbourhood in a deprived district of east London messaged him asking for money, unaware that in reality he was still living at home in his parents' house at the age of 30. The consequences of a culture that reveres prodigious achievement and encourages millions of us to curate a personal brand among our peers are that young adults and teenagers feel pressure to succeed as young as possible. For young men in particular this means acquiring vast material wealth. In an age of winners and losers, being a loser has become a moral failure, yet as more people turn to social media for their self-worth and livelihood, the biggest beneficiaries are the platforms who sell our attention.

The winners and the losers

If I tallied all the people I interviewed for this book who are generating a livelihood from their streams and selfies – Ebz, who is paid to be racially abused; Jessy, who had sex with a robot remote-controlled by alt right trolls; Cherrise, who is under constant pressure to modify her body to look like an Instagram filter – I struggle to count any as a winner, despite their moderate success in gaining paying followers. Workers once rallied around the call for 'an honest day's pay for an honest day's work'. It is open for debate what this represents in the influencer economy. What counts as fair pay, especially when the price paid includes a loss of dignity from the dehumanising and dishonest ways attention demands to be monetised? Far too often, gaining attention means appealing to the worst parts of the internet – or, more accurately, the worst instincts of humanity.

Even if I put any moral considerations to the side and count the winners of the attention economy by looking at their bank balance, there is still a glaring problem. YouTubers, Instagrammers and TikTok creators are all at the whim of the rules, payment models and algorithms of platforms they do not own, cannot control and upon which they are utterly reliant. They do not get a vote on how engagement should be counted or how easy it is to find their pages, and often they find themselves disadvantaged by arbitrary adjustments. In recent years, creators on YouTube have seen their income change every time the algorithm does, whether by amending the average length of videos they want to recommend, or through moderation software demonetising the videos of popular creators. The group who often find themselves most affected are those posting and selling erotic material.

Facebook's Instagram seems happy to use the public's sexual mores to grow its user base, and its algorithms often boost those selling their bodies in one way or another, but it will also come down on those individuals who contribute to its success. Instagram models with OnlyFans accounts will find their accounts shut down and have to start again. Influencers can see their income plummet if they do not stay up to date with how the platforms generate attention. Creators are vulnerable, and they know there is a thin line between winning the battle for the internet and being ejected altogether. The only certain winners are the tech companies disproportionately located on the West Coast of America.

California has long been a magnet for the ambitious and the entrepreneurial, even before it was part of the United States. It was the early Spanish settlers who christened the valleys 'California', after the fictional paradise in the novel *The Adventures of Esplandián*. Once gold was discovered, the non-native population of the area soared from an estimated 8,000 to 255,000 by the early 1850s. Within a century, the population was just under seven million; half of that number lived in San Francisco and the surrounding Bay Area alone.

The megacity and Los Angeles have almost single-handedly defined the modern California brand. Where most people in the world expect to die at the same status as they were born, California always appeared to offer a ladder. Today, it is the bona fide mecca of the attention industry, in which everyone is told they can prosper if they are willing to hustle. The beautiful and bombastic head to Los Angeles. The bright young things migrate to the Bay Area, the region between Palo Alto, Sunnyvale and San José that makes up San Francisco's so-called Silicon Valley. There they create the platforms the pretty young things in LA broadcast from. LA and San Francisco were once rivals with ideological conflicts, but now they form two sides of the world's influencer industry.

On my first visit to San Francisco, I found a city in both the future and the past. I was staying for the most part with a friend from London who had moved there with the dream of starting a company and taking it to a billion-dollar valuation – otherwise known as unicorn status. He believed the money was in California, and he had a good hand too. He was young, a graduate of the prestigious London School of Economics and a former analyst at the much-heralded global consultancy firm McKinsey. His was the kind of profile investors trust. To make matters even better, he was enrolled at Y Combinator, San Francisco's leading incubator for new start-ups, which connects graduates from the world's elite schools with a trough of rich investors.

On my visit, we hired a white Tesla, the somewhat self-driving electric car, and cruised around the company towns of Apple, Google and Facebook, the companies that have driven the attention economy by smashing the old media power brokers. So much of the digital world has been conceived in Palo Alto, the playground of the ambitious and the connected, a town that feels both moneyed and discreet. My friend had fantasised about running into Peter Thiel, the renowned investor and libertarian, on University Drive. This is the high street of coffee shops, sushi bars and fashionable eateries that leads up to Stanford University's grand campus. Thiel famously turned his $500,000 early investment in Facebook into over $1bn.[13]

But Palo Alto and the Bay Area don't have much of a centre to them beyond the university. You might conceivably run into a billionaire on the way to Starbucks, but most of the routes to money are closed without a guest pass. My friend had his, courtesy of his Y Combinator enrolment. But even so, after a few weeks he began to notice that those in his class were not there because of any great intelligence, but due to an ability to project confidence and sell it. 'They'll out-hustle you any day of the week,' he said. In the end, he reasoned, they were all just selling the future, and in truth, nobody knows what that looks like. The only answer is to be surer of your vision than anyone else.

Driving through the mazy city that is Stanford University, we passed the now infamous 1701 Page Mill Road. The building was HQ to Theranos, a health technology company founded by a young Stanford drop-out, Elizabeth Holmes, when she was just 19. She had managed to raise hundreds of millions of dollars with a story that she could revolutionise blood tests by taking less of our blood but learning more from it. She promised that blood taken from a pinprick could be analysed instantly, thanks to her invention, the Edison.

Holmes used social media and mainstream media to present herself as a genius heir to Silicon Valley legend Steve Jobs, and even modelled herself on the late Palo Alto native and Apple founder by adopting his trademark turtleneck. At its peak, her company was valued at $9bn. The only problem was that the technology she was selling did not yet exist, and the technology she did have did not do what she claimed. She had sold a fiction, marvellously chronicled by John Carreyrou in the book *Bad Blood* and turned into a hit Netflix documentary. In 2018, Holmes was indicted by a federal grand jury on nine counts of fraud.[14]

The impact of her fraud was still being felt when I visited the Bay Area in July 2019, but if the scandal was supposed to trigger a new way of doing things in Silicon Valley, that wasn't the vibe I was getting. For my friend launching his start-up there, Holmes's only mistake was managing expectations. He concluded that in the world of venture capitalism, a fiction is necessary to the hustle: 'There's a grey area between being a scammer and the person who actually changes health care. Those two worlds are a lot closer than you think.' If you have to sell your idea long before you have built it, then how do you avoid faking it until you make it? At the core of this logic is a delusional optimism, and if you fail, you just have to hope that no one is watching.

Billy McFarland's now infamous fraud with Fyre Festival was played out in front of millions. McFarland was a graduate of Y Combinator's East Coast rival, Dreamit, an accelerator that rewards promising start-ups with investor contacts and office space. He had joined the programme with his social media start-up, which sought to allow users to share music and video, forming circles of friends based on shared interests. When the ill-fated Google+ was launched with all of these features, McFarland searched for new pastures. He would go on to launch the now infamous Fyre Festival, the project that led to his six-year conviction for fraud.[15]

Then 25 years old, McFarland was unqualified and poorly prepared. He lied to both investors and consumers to make the festival (almost) happen. Yet had he pulled it off, he would have been celebrated as an entrepreneurial prodigy like WeWork founder Adam Neumann, who himself emerged as a yarn spinner. WeWork rented out prime office space to start-ups and corporates, but presented itself as a tech firm with a new paradigm. And it was treated like one by investors, who flooded it with cash, inflating its valuation to $47bn despite it never getting near a profit. Technology website Crunchbase wrote presciently that 'WeWork is valued more like a software company than a real estate firm. And that's going to be interesting to watch Wall Street tangle with.'

However, by 2019, when Neumann attempted to deposit the billions he now held on paper as WeWork began the process of going public, the scale of mismanagement and deception at the heart of the model began to be revealed. Neumann had exploited the company as a personal cash cow, with some dubious decisions. He had trademarked the 'We' part of the brand name and then leased it back to the company at a cost of $6m, and had even bought buildings that were then rented to the business.[16] In other words, he made millions as a landlord to his own company.[17] Furthermore, WeWork had missed its financial targets by almost $1bn. It was expensive to run, haemorrhaged money and was reliant on investors, like a Ponzi scheme without an easy road to profit. The company has become a symbol of the venture capital gravy train, where good-looking, charismatic elites in the image of billionaire investors are able to sell expensive lottery tickets with no guarantee that there is even a jackpot to be won.

Like Neumann, Obinwanne Okeke has graced the cover of *Forbes* magazine, when he was selected to be one of their 30 Under 30 rising stars in Africa for 2016, and was also prominent in the scene of rising Nigerian millennials. In the absence of a reliable welfare state, the country is bursting with entrepreneurs. The problem is that business in Nigeria is even more rigged than in the US. Success can be tied to family connections or patronage in a pool of limited patrons. Yet in one of the hardest places to make it, Okeke appeared to have done just that after curating a profile as a major influencer. The BBC's Veronica Edwards presented him as an 'inspiring entrepreneur' and broadcast his story to the world.

Okeke was already a prominent fixture in the Nigerian blogosphere. His wedding proposal featured on the lifestyle website BellaNaija that covers the ins and outs of Nigeria's biggest influencers. In his professional work, Okeke lobbied global investors to support his country's entrepreneurs, writing: 'Nigeria has the talent and potential to attract double what they currently do if there is a targeted policy to develop spaces for these tech incubators to thrive.' As he waited for the kind of life-changing investment that had made companies like WeWork successful, it was his fund-raising activities that were his undoing.

In 2019, Okeke landed on US soil and was arrested by the FBI at the airport for wire fraud. Unatrac, the UK subsidiary of the American heavy equipment manufacturer Caterpillar, had had $11m stolen via an email fraud that used a hoax company email to spoof officials. Okeke pleaded guilty. This fraud, widely committed by Nigerian gangs, is commonly known as 419, after the section of the country's penal code that tackles such crimes. Nigerian criminologist Oludayo Tade wrote on academic network the Conversation that 'the instability in the Nigerian banking sector may have created an uncommitted workforce. Working in an insecure establishment makes workers vulnerable. More than 2,000 bankers have lost their jobs due to economic recession in the country. A large number of casual workers are deployed to man key positions in the banks. This makes way for criminal opportunities.'

The novelist Adaobi Tricia Nwaubani has described Nigeria's internet scammers – known as yahoo boys – as the country's 'role models'. There are iconic songs about their lavish lifestyles, from the classic Afrobeat anthem 'Yahooze' to the new-wave 'Am I a Yahoo Boy' by Naira Marley, a pop star himself arrested for fraud. Nigeria's scam culture is mundane and ordinary. Everybody knows that society is rigged and those at the helm are notoriously corrupt, and so theft is seen as fair work in an unfair economy.

Many of the young educated men working in Nigeria's thriving fraud industry are intelligent, diligent and innovative problem-solvers trying to get rich or die trying because they live on the southside of the global economy. Had Okeke had the same opportunities as the founder of WeWork, he would have had better odds. Both he and Neumann had designs on breaking into the Davos elite and built elaborate mythologies around themselves to qualify. Both are charismatic seducers of people, with non-traditional backgrounds compared to their high-society rivals. Both misrepresented or manipulated their truths. However, the game of high-stakes snakes and ladders only rewards a handful of players, and for Okeke and his ilk, young men born into the wrong families, in the wrong places and in the wrong skin, there are more snakes than ladders.

In the UK, 92 per cent of recipients of major investment from the venture capital funds that enable businesses to succeed are male, and 90 per cent are white.[18] It is clear who is allowed to dream in an economy where fiction and hustle attract greater rewards than hard work. That is the lesson given to my generation, who graduated into the labour market in between two major crises, the 2008 financial crash and the COVID pandemic. And while the banks may have been the pantomime villains in 2008, since then the tech giants have been catching up as the popular purveyors of dishonesty and moneyed influence.

Google has a rap sheet that stretches back well over a decade. While building Street View in the early 2000s, the company used cars that appeared only to photograph streets and buildings whilst covertly capturing more than they announced. The vehicles were fitted with an antenna designed to scan local Wi-Fi networks and hoover up emails, passwords, adulterous conversations and other sensitive information from unsecured networks. When this was revealed following a data audit by Germany's data protection regulator, Google described it as the accidental mistake of a rogue engineer.[19] Emails later showed this to be misleading.[20] The engineer knew what he was doing and so did the company, according to a paper trail between him and his superiors.[21] Google was fined for being uncooperative with the watchdog.[22] In 2009, as the authorities began to crack down on the illegal mining of our data, Google was fined €1.49bn by the EU for advertising violations.[23]

In 2019, YouTube, owned by Google, was fined a record $170m by the US Federal Trade Commission for violating children's privacy laws and collecting the data of under-13s without parental consent.[24] Google had refused to acknowledge that part of its main YouTube service was directed at children, yet it was openly selling the attention of its young audience to multinational companies. The firm told Mattel, the manufacturer of Barbie, that 'YouTube is today's leader in reaching children aged 6–11 against top TV channels.'[25]

The influencers they watched were agents of a new monopoly, selling on our attention. Only Facebook comes close to its dominance.

Facebook has also been besieged by scandal in recent years. In 2019, it paid $5bn to resolve an investigation with the US Federal Trade Commission,[26] which alleged that it 'used deceptive disclosures and settings' and had obtained personal phone numbers for security but repurposed them to target advertisements. It also allegedly deceived 'tens of millions of users' by implying that a facial recognition feature on the service had not been enabled by default, when it had.

Facebook's grip on our attention had made it a major platform for mainstream media who had seen their audience decline. Between 2014 and 2018, many media outfits began pivoting to digital news, employing entire teams dedicated to cutting video for Facebook, where views were booming. At Channel 4 News in the UK, where I work, an ordinary story cut for Facebook could reach over 100 million views. In comparison, our audience watching the same story on TV would be between 500,000 and 900,000. Corporates also began spending more money on Facebook video. The company encouraged marketers to pay for more adverts and used their reach as an incentive for struggling media outlets to make higher-value content for the platform if they wanted the attention of Facebook's users.

But the high views viral videos seem to be achieving on the platform have been disputed. According to a class lawsuit from advertisers filed in 2018, Facebook was inflating the viewing numbers by as much as 900 per cent.[27] When they corrected the algorithm, viewing figures plummeted. In 2019, they agreed to pay $40m in settlement.[28] The media companies who had hired new teams to make news videos designed to reach people on Facebook now fired them.

The new attention barons have unprecedented power and in a single lifetime have made countless riches whilst breaking the law and covertly monitoring us. The surveillance of the internet by the Big Tech companies has been for one purpose: to know our thoughts before we do, so they can personalise adverts and sell our attention to the highest bidder. This industry has helped make California the fifth-ranked economy on the planet, at $3.1tn.[29] It is easier to count the major Western platforms that are not based in California than the ones that are. The companies headquartered in a small triangle of the Bay Area have more cash on hand than many sovereign nations. The wealthy workers flooding into San Francisco are driving the poor out of the city. The Bay is home to the new 1 per cent and the consequence has been one of the most severe rates of homelessness in America in a state built on an underclass of invisible migrant labour from Latin America.

Big Tech may make more money than anyone else, but if they continue not to replace anywhere near the jobs they have killed off, what do the rest of us do? A narrow class of elite graduates and world-class bullshitters with the right accents can compete for the favour of a rich investor or a few gilded jobs, but that road is not open to most. Despite the conviction that we can do anything we set our mind to, the truth is that in this economy so many of our life chances are determined by our circumstances. For your average Gen Z, joining a pyramid scheme or the attention hunger games as an aspiring influencer has become the most accessible route. On YouTube, Twitch, Instagram, TikTok and even Twitter, millennials and teenagers are mining their lives and identities for attention, income or advantage, using dishonesty wherever necessary. If the big companies at the top of the pyramid can deceive for profit without consequences, then it is not surprising that this attitude has trickled down in an economy where deception and spin are central to modern capitalism. And if this was true in 2019, COVID-19 has only amplified the trend and revealed how fragile rugged individualism is.

The scamdemic

I have one rule on New Year's Eve: stay home or stay within a 15-minute walk of home. Clubs on NYE are hellish and extortionate, and the streets of every major city, including my own, effectively shut down, tripling the length of cab journeys, which have already quadrupled in price. Throughout my twenties, I opted to throw house parties, which to be honest were thankfully legendary. Even so, the pressure to have a 'good' night is only surpassed by the pressure to have a 'happy' new year, increasingly defined by success. It was a pressure even more palpable on 31 December 2019, the eve of not just a new year but a new decade.

Even for the most ardent sceptic, NYE 2020 felt like a chance to say goodbye to a decade that had been divisive and unkind. My social media feeds were awash with hopeful memes hailing the return of the 'roaring twenties', along with the usual 'new year, new me' promises. The cheesy mantra #2020Vision sprang up everywhere and was tagged onto 1.9 million posts on Instagram. #2020Goals had 1.3 million. 2020, or twenty-twenty, had a phonetic symmetry that made it sound like a concept year from the future, or some kind of fancy government initiative, rather than an arbitrary number. The year had a sense of youthful possibility. The newly elected British prime minister Boris Johnson signed off 2019 with a message promising a 'fantastic year and a remarkable decade for our United Kingdom'.[30]

By April 2020, all of that optimism felt like a twisted joke, as the year started to resemble a second-rate dystopian thriller. A killer virus swept the earth, racking up over 50 million cases and a global death toll of over 2.7 million by

March 2021.[31] Even more people had lost their freedoms and their livelihoods. Half the world's population – 3.9 billion people[32] – had found themselves locked down by confinements or curfews, told by their governments to stay indoors to prevent the spread of the virus.[33]

In many parts of the world, industries like hospitality were effectively suspended, shops were closed, and major events such as the Olympics were cancelled. Overnight, millions were plunged below the breadline. Nearly 80 per cent of the two billion workers in the informal economy were at risk of losing their income, along with 305 million full-time workers.[34] Many around me lost their jobs, and even the editor of this book was temporarily placed on furlough in the UK government scheme that effectively paid 80 per cent of the salaries of the employees who were affected.

When China, the world's leading manufacturer, had shut down to deal with the virus, most outside the country assumed this wasn't our problem, but as the pandemic moved across the globe at breakneck speed, it became apparent that everyone everywhere was facing grave danger. The impact of the global lockdowns has been even more devastating than the 2008 banking crisis, shutting down our entire economic system. The severity of effectively banning citizens from leaving their homes to socialise, suspending banking services and international tourism, closing public spaces and shelving entire industries that were considered non-essential forced every major government to take over the running of its economy or risk it immediately collapsing. In the UK, on top of the furlough scheme, the government agreed to socialise the losses of major companies, underwrote entire sectors, offered businesses interest-free lines of credit, allowed mortgage holidays, suspended the housing market, banned evictions and wrote the National Health Service a blank cheque.

Similar measures applied across other developed economies. Canada even introduced a universal basic income in all but name, and Republicans remarkably debated doing the same in the US. The UK increased Universal Credit for those without an income, albeit not by much. In the 2019 election, the Conservative Party had called Labour's campaign pledge for free public broadband 'a crazy communist scheme'.[35] Months later, the government had made a U-turn as they worked with providers to improve services and cut costs as a matter of economic urgency now that so many people were required to work from home. The cost of underwriting the economy is still being tallied and is forecast to run into the trillions.

The emergency policies were an economic necessity. Central banks had already effectively made money free by slashing interest rates to almost 0 per cent to drive demand, but in doing so had left themselves with little ammunition. The only other way to spur demand is to literally give citizens cash to pump into the system, and across the world, many government schemes did just that. Prior to the crisis, most adults of working age were either over-leveraged on expensive mortgages – in the UK these were now over 10 times the average person's salary – or paying eye-watering rents. Younger millennials were drowning in student debt while earning less than their equivalents 20 years earlier.

With many billions invested by capitalists seeking high returns wasted on overhyped companies like WeWork, asset growth had lined the pockets of the 1 per cent but left the majority with little scope to absorb financial shocks. The coronavirus shutdown highlighted how insecure essential human necessities like housing and public health care had become, thanks to dysfunctional markets being driven by greed rather than need. In the US, 27.5 million people[36] were without health care as the pandemic struck, foreshadowing a potential economic Armageddon.

Ten years after I graduated into the aftermath of a banking crisis, I was finally preparing for middle-class adulthood. I had made an offer on a house in London and spent thousands on a home survey, the broker's fee and a lawyer just as the housing market was suspended. My partner and I were both fortunate to have jobs in the immediate lockdown, although my better half was issued with a pay cut by her company. It could have been worse and we were certainly part of a privileged minority. After the government announced the lockdown, almost a million people signed on to the Universal Credit scheme in the space of a week. Many of the country's five million self-employed people saw their income reduced to nothing.[37] For those under 40 and without assets, who had struggled since 2008, the economy had fucked them again.

But for all the uncertainty the lockdown brought, coronavirus created a reckoning for the way we live and work. The virus was spread by affluent jet-setters. The first major outbreak in Europe was in the Lombardy ski resorts a few hours away from the elite hangout of Davos. But soon the suspension of flights and the reduced use of cars meant that carbon and other toxic emissions plummeted. Coronavirus was bad for capitalism but seemed good for the planet. Until the virus, our economic life had been determined by confidence in continuous consumption and overproduction, even if at a huge social and environmental cost. We had to keep spending for the system to work. Suddenly, it was no longer clear if we were following the right path.

The pandemic also forced us to face the meaninglessness of modern work in an advanced economy, and the limits of individualism. The importance of public service and even low-paid jobs in core business sectors like food delivery and cleaning became unquestionable, and some fast-fashion influencers even began to reconsider promoting cheaply produced items for major polluters (although not for long). But if some felt guilty at posting trivial thirst traps for dubious brands, in other cases the money for these paid posts had dried up entirely. In the first business quarter of 2020, brands told influencers they were not planning to spend until the third quarter, and even then the landscape was changing. The number of deaths from coronavirus and the time spent in lockdown with limited freedom forced us all to consider the way we wanted to live our lives and the dishonesty of everyday economic existence.

Even major companies rethought their attitude to work. In 2020, Twitter told its employees that they would be able to work from home 'forever',[38] as an estimated 40 per cent of employees in developed economies have reported working from home effectively.[39] However, the question is just how many people will be in work at all after the fallout really begins to be felt. The number of people unemployed in the OECD – the world's advanced economies – rose by 18 million to 55 million in April 2020, and this was with government intervention.[40] Many of the newly jobless have migrated online. According to Jennifer Quigley-Jones, founder of the influencer agency Digital Voices, platforms like OnlyFans have grown exponentially, along with searches about how to edit YouTube videos and make money online. However, not every opportunity online is what it seems.

In the past decade the internet has gone from a millennial salvation to our financial damnation. Pyramid schemes disguised as employment have blossomed thanks to the immeasurable pressure to be rich, especially among young men and working-class racial minorities. The saturation of unobtainable wealth and luxury goods online has put a burden on young adults and teenagers to keep up with their peers. The longer you spend on Instagram, the more you are likely to believe that if you are not successful or wealthy then you are failing and need to get your money up: a boastful proverb of hip-hop culture that provides the dominant soundtrack for young adults and adolescents. The coronavirus shutdown showed how dependent success is on things outside of our control. Where you were born, when you were born and who you were born to are more powerful factors than your individual hustle, despite what the plethora of business coaches and DIY finance gurus teach the aspirational online.

The irony of the coronavirus crisis for influencer culture is that no event in memory has forced more people online. Those who could began working from home using digital tools, and moved all social activity to apps like Houseparty, Clubhouse and Zoom. Even my mum, who previously had no presence online, set up an Instagram account to stay connected to her church while the building was forced to close. The big winners, of course, were the social media companies, who saw record profits. Yet despite social media taking up more of our attention, our time trapped there reveals its limits in providing a good livelihood and a healthy way to live. As our way of life resumes post-pandemic, we have to ask ourselves what constitutes a good life and an economy that delivers happiness and security for the greatest number of people. Until this is resolved, the emphasis on individual wealth and prodigious overnight success at a time of income insecurity will continue to combine with social media platforms to reward dishonesty.

In the coronavirus shutdown, some of the most diligent digital hustlers were finding it easier to sell dreams. My Instagram feed became even more saturated with micro-influencers peddling get-rich schemes disguised as help, and sharing hustle memes telling followers that 'If you don't come out of this quarantine with a new skill, your side hustle started, more knowledge, you never lacked time, you lacked discipline.' One young woman who was slowly making her way up the ladder of the network marketing company IM Mastery Academy posted the following:

Two weeks of quarantine?

Working from home?

Why not make another source of income?

This is the best time to learn a skill and get paid from the largest financial market …

The message ended with an option to find out more, and a friendly animation labelled 'Quarantine & Chill'. With job insecurity and precarious work on the rise, it was only a matter of time before somebody clicked 'Tell me more'.

ACKNOWLEDGEMENTS

I would first like to thank Elizabeth Pears for her love and support in producing this work, my agent Nicola Chang for developing the story I wanted to tell and my editor Mike Harpley for his astute reader's eye. I am most thankful to everybody who made the time to speak to me, notably Daisy Gonzalez and Marissa Nuncio at the Garment Workers Centre in California and the brave workers who shared their stories. I am grateful to this book's larger than life characters: Rose, Ebenezer, Jessy, Cherrise, Des Amey, Joel Contartese, Hank and John Green, Suzie McFadden, Jenny Quigley-Jones and Tarla Makaeff.

I am grateful for the reflection, time or endorsements of my early readers: Reni Eddo-Lodge, Yomi Adegoke, Jason Okundaye, Moya Lothian-McLean, Emma Dabiri, Sara Willis, Marja Möller, Iman Amrani, Lyn Munroe, Ola Masha and Vicky Spratt. I am also thankful for the comradeship of Nels Abbey, Elijah Lawal and Derek Owusu whose experiences of publishing prepared the ground for me. Andrew Rajanathan, Nathan Edwards and Hila May also made vital contributions with interviewees, ideas or leads. I would also like to thank the readers of the hardback who have shared it, reviewed it or recommended it. In an age of infinite content, it is a great privilege to have any readers at all. Thank you.

REFERENCES

Introduction: The Hustler's Ambition

1. https://thesource.com/2017/02/06/50-cent-releases-get-rich-or-die-tryin-14-years-ago/
2. https://twitter.com/AllThatandMoore/status/1009432296703840258/retweets/with_comments; and https://www.complex.com/music/2019/01/i-think-i-got-souljascammed
3. https://www.youtube.com/watch?v=Kp5A_1UAJog
4. https://www.forbes.com/sites/brianpetchers/2014/08/13/soulja-boys-blueprint-to-success-and-the-next-chapter/?sh=1c07f6a73b73
5. http://news.bbc.co.uk/1/hi/uk_politics/460009.stm
6. https://researchbriefings.files.parliament.uk/documents/SN04252/SN04252.pdf
7. https://www.bbc.co.uk/news/uk-politics-40965479
8. https://dera.ioe.ac.uk/6778/1/reach-report.pdf
9. https://www.fenews.co.uk/press-releases/20673-news-story-education-secretary-launches-24-million-programme-for-north-east
10. https://www.kering.com/en/news/record-operating-margin-sustained-growth-trajectory#:~:text=In%202019%2C%20Kering%20had%20over,revenue%20of%20%E2%82%AC15.9%20billion
11. https://www.theguardian.com/fashion/2017/jul/11/glitz-glamour-tragedy-how-gianni-versace-rewrote-rules-fashion

12. https://www.weforum.org/agenda/2020/08/apples-stock-market-value-tops-2-trillion/
13. https://themobmuseum.org/blog/colombian-drug-lord-pablo-escobar-spent-seven-years-on-forbes-list-of-worlds-richest/#:~:text=In%20July%201989%2C%20Escobar%20made,list%20for%20seven%20consecutive%20years
14. https://www.bbc.co.uk/newsround/49124484
15. https://www.ft.com/content/81343d9e-187b-11e8-9e9c-25c814761640
16. https://www.theguardian.com/society/2016/jul/18/millennials-earn-8000-pounds-less-in-their-20s-than-predecessors
17. https://www.theguardian.com/money/2018/feb/16/homeownership-among-young-adults-collapsed-institute-fiscal-studies

Chapter 1: The Unicorn in Polyester

1. https://www.refinery29.com/en-us/2019/02/224802/kim-kardashian-fashion-nova-mugler-dress
2. Ibid.
3. https://wwd.com/fashion-news/fashion-features/inside-fashion-nova-cardi-b-1202595964/
4. https://publications.parliament.uk/pa/cm201719/cmselect/cmenvaud/1952/1952.pdf
5. https://publications.parliament.uk/pa/cm201719/cmselect/cmenvaud/1952/report-files/195204.htm
6. Ibid.

Chapter 2: Under the Knife

1. https://baaps.org.uk/about/news/1630/the_bottom_line/
2. https://www.dailymail.co.uk/news/article-8952335/

British-office-worker-47-died-having-4-300-boob-job-Turkey-secretly-resuscitated.html

3. https://www.bbc.co.uk/news/av/health-55596969

Chapter 3: Find Some Fans

1. https://www.theinformation.com/articles/onlyfans-chief-talks-sports-ambitions-and-role-of-adult-content-in-site
2. https://www.bloomberg.com/news/articles/2020-12-05/celebrities-like-cardi-b-could-turn-onlyfans-into-a-billion-dollar-media-company
3. https://thefword.org.uk/2016/04/middle-classing/

Chapter 4: Smile (or Fight), You're on Camera

1. https://www.green-card.com/how-high-are-the-chances-of-winning/#:~:text=The%20average%20chance%20of%20winning,rise%20again%20to%201%3A25!
2. https://www.newyorker.com/magazine/2018/07/09/ice-poseidons-lucrative-stressful-life-as-a-live-streamer
3. https://www.bbc.co.uk/news/technology-28930781
4. https://www.bbc.co.uk/news/newsbeat-29404364
5. https://www.youtube.com/watch?v=FMzjm8BG8cU
6. https://variety.com/2013/digital/news/youtube-standardizes-ad-revenue-split-for-all-partners-but-offers-upside-potential-1200786223/
7. https://www.statista.com/statistics/266249/advertising-revenue-of-google/#:~:text=In%202020%2C%20Google's%20ad%20revenue%20amounted%20to%20146.92%20billion%20US%20dollars.
8. https://www.bloomberg.com/news/articles/2020-02-04/instagram-generates-more-than-a-quarter-of-facebook-s-sales

9. https://investor.fb.com/investor-news/press-release-details/2021/Facebook-Reports-Fourth-Quarter-and-Full-Year-2020-Results/default.aspx

10. https://www.reuters.com/article/us-bytedance-tiktok-exclusive-idUSKCN24U1M9

Chapter 5: Work From Home: Ask Me How

1. https://www.theguardian.com/business/2020/jul/30/amazon-apple-facebook-google-profits-earnings

2. https://www.businessinsider.com/is-it-works-legit-2015-8?r=US&IR=T

3. https://itworks.com/Legal/Income/

4. https://www.census.gov/library/publications/2020/demo/p60-270.html

5. https://www.glassdoor.co.uk/Reviews/Employee-Review-It-Works-Global-RVW14986048.htm

6. Ibid.

7. https://www.buzzfeednews.com/article/stephaniemcneal/lularoe-millennial-women-entrepreneurship-lawsuits

8. https://www.bloomberg.com/news/features/2018-04-27/thousands-of-women-say-lularoe-s-legging-empire-is-a-scam

9. Ibid.

10. https://www.yahoo.com/lifestyle/leaked-comments-lularoe-ceo-ignite-controversy-214640143.html

11. https://www.atg.wa.gov/news/news-releases/lularoe-pay-475-million-resolve-ag-ferguson-s-lawsuit-over-pyramid-scheme

12. Ibid.

13. https://www.bloomberg.com/news/features/2018-04-27/thousands-of-women-say-lularoe-s-legging-empire-is-a-scam

14. Jia Tolentino, *Trick Mirror* (Fourth Estate, 2019)
15. Stephen Gilpin, *Trump U: The Inside Story of Trump University* (OR Books, 2018)
16. https://www.nbcnews.com/politics/white-house/federal-court-approves-25-million-trump-university-settlement-n845181
17. Gilpin, op. cit.
18. https://www.theguardian.com/us-news/2016/jun/01/trump-university-staff-testimony-fraudulent-scheme
19. Gilpin, op. cit.
20. Ibid.
21. Ibid.
22. https://www.theguardian.com/us-news/2016/jun/01/trump-university-staff-testimony-fraudulent-scheme
23. https://ag.ny.gov/press-release/2018/ag-schneiderman-statement-final-trump-university-settlement
24. https://bossbabe.com/
25. https://www.ft.com/content/c2114610-770f-11e9-b0ec-7dff87b9a4a2

Chapter 6: The Art of the Hack

1. https://www.theguardian.com/technology/2020/mar/18/facebook-says-spam-filter-mayhem-not-related-to-coronavirus
2. https://www.shopifyandyou.com/blogs/news/statistics-about-shopify#:~:text=More%20than%201.2%20million%20people%20are%20actively%20using%20the%20Shopify%20backend%20platform.
3. https://www.youtube.com/watch?v=pIMiazcR96E&lc=UgionhuqPuvbgHgCoAEC
4. https://www.youtube.com/watch?v=iDfl2khJK1g
5. https://unctad.org/press-material/global-e-commerce-hits-256-trillion-latest-unctad-estimates

6. https://internetretailing.net/industry/industry/uk-ecommerce-accounts-for-19-of-total-retail-making-it-worth-233bn-20971

7. https://www.theinformation.com/articles/people-follow-people-and-other-themes-on-the-creator-economy?utm_source=ti_app

Chapter 7: Outsider Trading

1. https://www.dailyecho.co.uk/news/15554405.self-proclaimed-millionaire-elijah-oyefeso-mowed-down-man-he-owed-money-in-southampton-street/

2. As of 13 March 2021

3. https://www.fca.org.uk/news/press-releases/fca-warns-increased-risk-online-investment-fraud-investors-scamsmart#:~:text=While%20historically%20over%2055s%20have,with%20over%2055s%20(2%25).

4. https://www.actionfraud.police.uk/news/fca-warns-public-of-investment-scams-as-over-197-million-reported-losses-in-2018; https://www.actionfraud.police.uk/news/action-fraud-warns-of-rise-in-investment-fraud-reports-as-nation-enters-second-lockdown

5. Companies House

6. https://www.reuters.com/article/us-crypto-currency-tesla-tweets-idUSKBN2A82F0

7. https://www.bloomberg.com/news/articles/2017-12-08/the-bitcoin-whales-1-000-people-who-own-40-percent-of-the-market

8. https://www.vox.com/2018/4/24/17275202/bitcoin-scam-cryptocurrency-mining-pump-dump-fraud-ico-value

9. https://www.sec.gov/investor/alerts/ia_virtualcurrencies.pdf

10. https://www.cftc.gov/system/files/2019/04/24/2018afr.pdf

11. https://neironix.io/documents/whitepaper/3914/Yield-Coin-Whitepaper-V4.compressed.pdf

12. Companies House

13. https://www.fca.org.uk/news/warnings/international-markets-live-limited

14. According to the Instagram of Alex Morton, one of the company's senior marketers, with over 1 million followers

15. https://www.forbes.com/sites/helaineolen/2012/10/10/rich-dad-poor-dad-bankrupt-dad/?sh=45bd6bc1633a

16. https://www.nber.org/system/files/chapters/c12624/c12624.pdf

17. https://www.federalreserve.gov/pubs/feds/2008/200859/200859pap.pdf

18. https://www.ft.com/content/bb1b9c50-e324-11dd-a5cf-0000779fd2ac

19. https://neweconomics.opendemocracy.net/time-call-housing-crisis-really-largest-transfer-wealth-living-memory/

20. https://webcache.googleusercontent.com/search?q=cache:IEtmBgbqZ6kJ:https://www.imarketslive.com/htdocs/IML-IDS.xlsx+&cd=3&hl=en&ct=clnk&gl=uk

21. https://www.rollingstone.com/culture/culture-news/selling-the-bro-dream-are-frat-boys-peddling-vemma-suckers-190425/

22. https://www.ftc.gov/news-events/blogs/business-blog/2016/12/dismantling-pyramid-lessons-vemma-settlement

23. https://www.ftc.gov/news-events/press-releases/2016/12/vemma-agrees-ban-pyramid-scheme-practices-settle-ftc-charges

24. Ibid.

25. Videos on Instagram

Chapter 8: Black Lives Matter, Here's My Ca$h App

1. https://www.huffingtonpost.co.uk/entry/lili-reinhart-breonna-taylor-justice_n_5efb9341c5b612083c53ec2c?ri18n=true

2. https://eu.usatoday.com/videos/news/nation/2019/09/13/cardi-b-supports-shaun-king/2309093001/

3. https://variety.com/2019/biz/news/shaun-king-and-mia-mottley-rihanna-diamond-ball-1203309460/

4. https://www.theroot.com/friend-foe-or-fraud-shaun-king-on-the-accusations-aga-1838042089

5. https://thegrio.com/2019/09/17/how-the-shaun-king-deray-mckesson-beef-leaves-us-not-knowing-what-to-think/?fbclid=IwAR033pkvGPqO5E8yKwM--her8a4wHjWqaBMfcV9kk6MYvoeylbiwmvbGx7k

6. https://www.essence.com/news/mother-of-tamir-rice-tells-activists-to-stop-profiting-off-her-sons-death/

7. https://www.dailymail.co.uk/news/article-9479179/BLM-founder-defends-property-empire-reveals-spent-week-security.html

8. https://www.nytimes.com/2019/08/21/business/popeyes-chicken-sandwich-twitter.html

9. https://www.agencedada.com/en/2019/12/11/popeyes-chicken-sandwich/

10. https://www.youtube.com/watch?v=eoP4KuKOIuM

11. https://www.spellmagazine.co.uk/spellmeets/meet-the-millennial-mastermind

12. https://www.self.com/story/ashley-grahams-body-revolution

13. https://www.merkleinc.com/emea/thought-leadership/white-papers/why-millennial-women-buy

14. https://novaramedia.com/2021/01/20/the-slumflower-beef-has-exposed-the-limits-of-influencer-activism/

15. https://www.bbc.co.uk/news/uk-39181532

16. https://www.thetimes.co.uk/article/why-should-i-worry-about-male-suicides-says-feminist-writer-rvjzq3xj8

17. https://www.vox.com/2018/9/26/17900890/twitter-instagram-scam-viral

18. https://www.linkedin.com/in/jacob-castaldi-917608100/

19. https://samsedlackcreative.com/about/

20. https://apnews.com/article/2d0e128733c99e78a81b962544
    dbf5f0

Conclusion: We Are All Influencers Now

1. https://www.asa.org.uk/news/how-many-followers-makes-
   a-celebrity-medicines-and-influencer-marketing.html
2. https://www.statista.com/statistics/951875/instagram-
   accounts-by-audience-size-share/
3. https://www.cbo.gov/sites/default/files/cbofiles/attachments/
   44256_TARP.pdf
4. https://fullfact.org/economy/1-trillion-not-spent-bailing-
   out-banks/
5. https://www.bbc.co.uk/news/business-29227597
6. https://www.bankofengland.co.uk/monetary-policy/
   quantitative-easing
7. https://www.reuters.com/article/us-greece-unemployment-
   idUSBRE9480EZ20130509
8. https://www.ifs.org.uk/publications/14508
9. https://www.ifs.org.uk/publications/8593; https://www.ifs.
   org.uk/publications/14949
10. https://www.bankofengland.co.uk/boeapps/database/Bank-
    Rate.asp
11. https://landregistry.data.gov.uk/app/ukhpi/browse?from=
    1990-01-01&location=http%3A%2F%2Flandregistry.data.
    gov.uk%2Fid%2Fregion%2Funited-kingdom&to=2017-
    12-01&lang=en
12. https://www.cambridge.org/core/journals/the-british-
    journal-of-psychiatry/article/trends-in-generalised-anxiety-
    disorders-and-symptoms-in-primary-care-uk-populationbased-
    cohort-study/5A04D331090B1CFB889ECDA8B8250D51
13. https://www.cnbc.com/2017/11/22/peter-thiel-sells-majority-
    of-facebook-shares-but-2012-was-bigger.html

14. https://www.justice.gov/usao-ndca/us-v-elizabeth-holmes-et-al

15. https://www.bloomberg.com/news/articles/2017-08-30/how-a-black-card-wannabe-went-down-in-flames

16. https://www.businessinsider.com/how-wework-paid-adam-neumann-59-million-to-use-the-name-we-2019-8?inline-read-more&r=US&IR=T

17. https://www.bloomberg.com/opinion/articles/2019-01-16/wework-ceo-adam-neumann-is-also-a-landlord

18. https://sifted.eu/articles/uk-founders-socioeconomic-privilege/

19. https://www.ft.com/content/db664044-6f43-11df-9f43-00144feabdc0

20. https://www.theguardian.com/technology/2012/apr/30/google-street-view-breach-fcc

21. https://venturebeat.com/2012/04/28/fcc-google-street-view-data/

22. https://www.scribd.com/fullscreen/91652398

23. https://ec.europa.eu/commission/presscorner/detail/en/IP_19_1770

24. https://www.ftc.gov/news-events/press-releases/2019/09/google-youtube-will-pay-record-170-million-alleged-violations

25. Ibid.

26. https://www.ftc.gov/news-events/press-releases/2019/07/ftc-imposes-5-billion-penalty-sweeping-new-privacy-restrictions

27. https://www.theverge.com/2018/10/17/17989712/facebook-inaccurate-video-metrics-inflation-lawsuit

28. https://www.documentcloud.org/documents/6455498-Facebooksettlement.html

29. https://www.forbes.com/places/ca/?sh=19b792763fef

30. https://news.sky.com/story/boris-johnson-promises-decade-of-prosperity-in-new-years-message-11898830

31. https://www.who.int/emergencies/diseases/novel-coronavirus-2019

32. https://www.economist.com/graphic-detail/2020/04/17/coronavirus-infections-have-peaked-in-much-of-the-rich-world

33. https://www.euronews.com/2020/04/02/coronavirus-in-europe-spain-s-death-toll-hits-10-000-after-record-950-new-deaths-in-24-hou

34. https://www.cnbc.com/2020/04/29/coronavirus-nearly-half-the-global-workforce-at-risk-of-losing-income.html

35. https://www.reuters.com/article/us-britain-election-bt-johnson/crazed-communist-scheme-pm-johnson-says-of-corbyns-plan-for-bt-idINKBN1XP1ER

36. https://www.census.gov/library/publications/2019/demo/p60-267.html

37. https://www.ons.gov.uk/employmentandlabourmarket/peopleinwork/employmentandemployeetypes/articles/coronavirusandselfemploymentintheuk/2020-04-24

38. https://www.bbc.co.uk/news/technology-52628119

39. https://ec.europa.eu/jrc/sites/jrcsh/files/jrc120945_policy_brief_-_covid_and_telework_final.pdf

40. https://www.oecd.org/newsroom/unemployment-rates-oecd-update-june-2020.htm#:~:text=09%2F06%2F2020%20%2D%20The,to%2055%20million%20in%20April.

INDEX

INDEX

INDEX